CHATELAINE
food express

Quickies 2

D1609144

CHATELAINE food express

Quickies 2

veggies and more

EASY WAYS WITH VEGETABLES, BEANS & GRAINS

BY MONDA ROSENBERG

M&S

A SMITH SHERMAN BOOK
produced in conjunction with CHATELAINE®
and published by McCLELLAND & STEWART INC.

CHATELAINE

Canadian Cataloguing in Publication Data

Rosenberg, Monda
    Quickies 2: veggies and more

(Chatelaine food express)
"A Smith Sherman book produced in conjunction with Chatelaine"
Includes index

ISBN 0-7710-7593-6

1. Cookery (Vegetables) 2. Cookery (Beans) 3. Cookery (Cereals)
4. Quick and easy cookery I. Title II. Series
TX801.R672 1999   641.5'55   C99-930242-6

ACKNOWLEDGEMENTS

Few in life are lucky enough to find a team of workmates they feel privileged to be associated with. I've been blessed in this regard both in my collaboration with Smith Sherman Books Inc. in producing the Food Express series of cookbooks and in my association with my colleagues at CHATELAINE magazine. I owe great appreciation to Carol Sherman and Andrew Smith, who massage and manipulate our recipes into such appealing and beautiful books. Thanks to Joseph Gisini for his meticulous attention to layout and design, Bernice Eisenstein for her flawless copy editing and Erik Tanner for all his input and help.
My sincere thanks also to the CHATELAINE Test Kitchen team, spearheaded by Marilyn Bentz Crowley and Trudy Patterson, who tested every recipe until they simply could not be improved upon; Deborah Aldcorn for her hawk-eyed editing; Editor Rona Maynard for her constant caring and input; Lee Simpson and Cheryl Smith for their strong commitment to this project; the CHATELAINE creative team of art director Caren Watkins and creative associate Barb Glaser; our world-class team of photographer Ed O'Neil, creative director Miriam Gee and food stylist Rosemarie Superville. Thanks to the entire McClelland & Stewart family, particularly editor Pat Kennedy for her constant support; and Alison Fryer and Jennifer Grange from the Cookbook Store for their sage advice.

MONDA ROSENBERG

COVER PHOTO: HEARTY HARVEST STEW, *see recipe page 101*

PHOTO PAGE 2: EGGPLANT STEAKS WITH CHÈVRE & TOMATOES, *see recipe page 41*

PHOTO PAGE 8: MUSHROOM RISOTTO, *see recipe page 69*

CREDITS: *see page 144*   PRINTED AND BOUND IN CANADA

AN A TO Z RECIPE BOOK STARRING VEGETABLES, GRAINS AND BEANS

Over the past decade we've learned to appreciate vegetables not just as sidekicks to the all-important entrée, but for their own outstanding garden-fresh flavors and appealing and ever-changing textures. At the same time, vegetables have gained superstar nutritional status, as study after study has raved about their benefits.

Today, more and more households boast at least one vegetarian, while many people are becoming almost vegetarians — eating less meat and more vegetables, grains and beans. In *Quickies 2*, with its emphasis on Veggies and more, we present easy and fast ways to bring this healthy fare to your table, whether it's a one-minute dressup for broccoli or a substantial tortilla lasagna for a vegetarian dinner.

The A to Z listing of ingredients established in the best-selling *Quickies* returns, with more than 25 categories, including asparagus, broccoli and carrots as well as some new additions such as cornmeal, for warm jalapeño-spiked bread and yummy polenta; greens, with four pages of recipes to keep you in salad days and xtras for avocados, parsnips and sugar snap peas. A popular vegetable such as tomato weighs in with more than 20 recipes. Broccoli, potatoes and rice have more than 15 recipes each. And again, as in *Quickies*, you will probably have many of the ingredients on hand. Eight pages in the Seasonal Guide provide tips for storing and cooking vegetables all year long. We've even included an All-Purpose Vegetable Broth (see recipe page 9).

Quickies 2 presents more than 300 recipes for the vegetarian teenager, the almost-vegetarian adult and anyone looking for new ways to spruce up their everyday vegetables.

A is for Artichokes . . .

CONTENTS

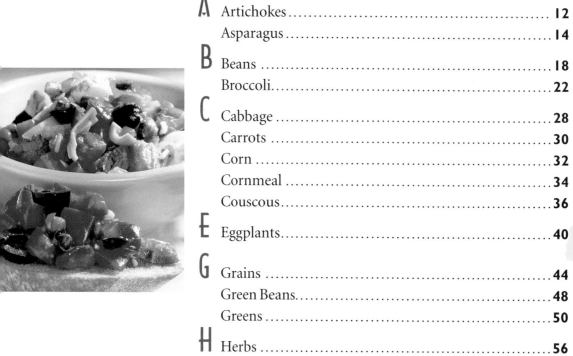

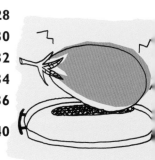

E is for Eggplants . . .

G is for Greens . . .

L is for Lemons . . .

R is for Rice . . .

S is for Squash . . .

ALL-PURPOSE VEGETABLE BROTH

A good vegetable broth goes a long way toward adding a depth of flavor to a world of vegetarian dishes. When made properly, it can be used interchangeably with chicken broth or stock and provide the flavor base for grand vegetarian entrées such as the Mushroom Risotto pictured here (see recipe page 69) or paellas, couscous and soups.

So search your vegetable bin. You can use vegetables that are beyond their prime, but still okay for consumption. Cooking water from peas, corn or carrots can be added. However, abandoned potato water does not cut it. Mild vegetables are more desirable, while strong turnips or parsnips are too assertive. And use a coffee filter as strainer to achieve a clear broth.

Coarsely chop or slice 1 large onion, 3 carrots, 2 stalks celery, including leaves, and 1 large trimmed leek. Finely chop 6 large garlic cloves.

Heat 1 tbsp oil in a large saucepan. Add all the vegetables and garlic. Stir frequently over medium heat for 5 min. Increase heat to high and stir constantly to lightly brown the vegetables for flavor.

As soon as the vegetables start to brown, after about 3 min., add 12 cups of water, 2 tsp salt, ½ tsp whole black peppercorns, 10 whole sprigs parsley and 1 bay leaf. Cover. When boiling, reduce heat to low and simmer, covered, for 1 hour.

Strain out all vegetables. Stock can be used right away, refrigerated for up to 4 days or frozen. *Makes 12 cups.*

A is for Artichokes . . . .

Chunky marinated artichokes pair with fresh
tomatoes to create an instant sophisticated nibble in
TOMATO & ARTICHOKE APPETIZER (see recipe page 12).
Pile this piquant mixture on baguettes,
crisp crackers or tortilla triangles.

A
B
C
D
E
F
G
H
I
J
K
L
M
N
O
P
Q
R
S
T
U
V
W
X
Y
Z

ARTICHOKES

Whether you buy them fresh or marinated, artichokes are a snap to prepare.
Use their addictive flavor to highlight appetizers, salads or pastas.

TOMATO & ARTICHOKE APPETIZER

Into a bowl, drain liquid from
    6-oz (170-mL) jar marinated artichokes.
Stir in 8 coarsely chopped seeded
    plum tomatoes, 1 minced garlic clove,
    2 tsp coarsely chopped capers,
    ½ cup pitted black olives and
    ¼ cup chopped coriander.
Coarsely chop artichokes and stir in.
Spoon onto slices of baguettes. Also good
    on crisp crackers. *Makes 5 cups.*

ARTICHOKE & PIMENTO QUICHE

Preheat oven to 425°F (220°C).
Scatter a 9-in. (23-cm) unbaked pie shell
    with 6-oz (170-mL) jar drained
    marinated artichoke hearts,
    cut into ½-in. (1-cm) pieces.
Sprinkle with 2 tbsp chopped pimento and
    1½ cups grated old cheddar.
Whisk 1½ cups homogenized milk with
    4 eggs and pinches of salt and pepper.
Pour into pie shell placed on a baking sheet.
    Bake on bottom rack for 10 min.
Reduce temperature to 350°F (180°C)
    and bake until centre of quiche seems
    set when jiggled, 25 to 30 min.
Serve warm. *Serves 6.*

ARTICHOKE & FETA PASTA

Cook 1 lb (450 g) penne until al dente,
    about 10 min.
Stir 6-oz (170-mL) jar undrained
    marinated artichokes with
    1½ cups small halved cherry tomatoes,
    1 cup crumbled feta,
    ¼ cup sliced pitted black olives,
    1 tsp dried basil, ½ tsp dried oregano,
    2 minced garlic cloves and
    generous grindings of black pepper.
Toss with hot drained pasta. Serve hot or
    at room temperature. *Serves 6 to 8.*

STEAMED FRESH ARTICHOKES

Trim base from 6 large artichokes.
    Pull off browned petals.
Place artichokes upright on a
    rack in a saucepan containing
    2 in. (5 cm) boiling salted water and
    2 tbsp freshly squeezed lemon juice.
Steam, covered, until bases can be pierced
    easily with a fork, from 20 to 25 min.
    Drain artichokes upside down.
Melt ½ cup butter with 3 tbsp freshly
    squeezed lemon juice.
Stir in 2 tbsp finely chopped coriander
    and pinches of salt and cayenne.
Use as a dipping sauce. *Serves 6.*

12

GLORIOUS GARLIC GREENS

Tear 1 head Boston lettuce and
  1 bunch arugula into bite-size pieces
  and toss with 2 (14-oz/398-mL) cans
  drained halved artichoke hearts.
Whisk 2 to 3 minced garlic cloves with
  ¼ cup olive oil, 2 tbsp red wine vinegar,
  ½ tsp Dijon and ¼ tsp each salt,
  pepper and sugar.
Toss with greens. Scatter with 1 cup black olives
  and 1 sliced red onion. *Serves 6 to 8.*

SPLENDID ITALIAN SALAD

In a food processor, whirl ½ cup olive oil,
  ¼ cup drained oil-packed sun-dried
  tomatoes, 3 minced garlic cloves,
  3 tbsp balsamic or red wine vinegar,
  ½ tsp each dried rosemary and basil and
  ¼ tsp pepper.
Tear 2 heads romaine lettuce into bite-size
  pieces. Drizzle about two-thirds of
  dressing over lettuce.
Scatter 14-oz (398-mL) can drained
  quartered artichokes and
  ½ cup black olives over top.
Toss and add more dressing if needed.
  Sprinkle with ½ cup shaved Parmesan.
  Serves 8 to 10.

QUICK MICROWAVE FRESH ARTICHOKES

Trim base from 4 artichokes.
  Stand in a microwave-safe dish.
Add ½ cup water and 1 tbsp freshly
  squeezed lemon juice.
Microwave, covered, on high until bases
  are fork-tender, from 13 to 18 min.
  Cover and let stand for 5 min.
Meanwhile, combine in a microwave bowl
  ⅓ cup butter, 1 tbsp freshly squeezed
  lemon juice, 2 tbsp finely chopped parsley
  and pinches of salt and pepper.
Microwave on high until melted, about 1 min.
Dip artichoke leaves in butter sauce. *Serves 4.*

SESAME-GINGER ARTICHOKE SALAD

Whisk ¼ cup vegetable oil with
  1 tbsp each sesame oil and soy sauce,
  2 tbsp lime juice, 2 minced garlic cloves,
  ¼ tsp minced fresh ginger, ¼ tsp sugar
  (optional) and pinch of cayenne.
Toss with 2 cups cold cooked Oriental noodles,
  14-oz (398-mL) can drained quartered
  artichoke hearts and ¼ cup chopped
  pimento or roasted red pepper. *Serves 4.*

Splendid Italian Salad

ASPARAGUS

Early spring marks the arrival of the beguiling asparagus.
Buy smooth stalks with closed compact tips.
Before cooking, break off pulpy portion at bottom of spears.

SPRING VEGGIE SAUTÉ

Cook 1 lb (454 g) baby carrots in boiling
   salted water for 3 min.
Add 2 bunches asparagus, diagonally sliced
   into 2-in. (5-cm) pieces and cook, 2 min.
Heat 1 tbsp each butter and olive oil in a large
   frying pan. Add 1 thinly sliced red onion
   and 2 minced garlic cloves. Sauté until
   soft, about 5 min.
Add drained carrots and asparagus and sauté
   for 2 min. Add salt and pepper. *Serves 8.*

ORIENTAL ASPARAGUS

Boil 1 lb (500 g) asparagus, covered, until
   tender-crisp, 4 min.
Whisk 1 tsp sesame oil with 1 tsp soy sauce,
   1 tsp grated orange or lemon peel and
   generous pinches of salt and white pepper.
Drain asparagus and arrange on a platter.
   Drizzle with dressing. *Serves 2 to 4.*

MICROWAVE GINGER-BUTTER ASPARAGUS

Trim ends from 1 lb (500 g) asparagus.
   Lay in a pinwheel pattern on a pie plate,
   overlapping tips in centre.
Add 1 tbsp water. Microwave, covered, on
   high, until tender-crisp, from 3 to 5 min.
Then microwave 1 tbsp butter with
   1 tsp freshly squeezed lemon juice,
   $\frac{1}{2}$ tsp finely minced fresh ginger and
   pinches of salt and pepper until melted,
   about 30 sec. Drizzle over asparagus.
   Serves 4.

ASPARAGUS WITH SAFFRON

Line a sieve with cheesecloth or large coffee
   filter and place over a bowl. Pour
   2 cups plain yogurt into cloth. Cover
   and let stand at room temperature for
   30 min. or in the refrigerator overnight.
Place thickened yogurt in a bowl, discarding
   liquid. Stir in 2 tsp honey mustard,
   pinch of crushed saffron and $\frac{1}{4}$ tsp cumin.
Boil 2 lbs (1 kg) asparagus, covered, until
   tender-crisp, 4 to 6 min.
Serve hot or at room temperature topped
   with saffron-yogurt sauce. *Serves 8.*

LIGHT & CREAMY PASTA SALAD

Diagonally slice 1 lb (500 g) asparagus
   into $\frac{1}{2}$-in. (1-cm) pieces.
Cook 1 lb (450 g) penne or rotini in boiling
   salted water until al dente, about 8 min.
Stir in asparagus. Continue boiling, 1 to 2 min.
Whisk 1 cup light sour cream with
   $\frac{1}{2}$ cup each light mayonnaise and 2% milk,
   1 tbsp Dijon, 2 minced garlic cloves and
   $\frac{1}{2}$ tsp each salt and pepper.
Stir in hot drained pasta and asparagus,
   4 chopped seeded plum tomatoes or
   2 large tomatoes and 1 cup shredded
   fresh basil or $1\frac{1}{2}$ tsp dried basil.
   Serves 6 to 8.

SPRING PASTA TOSS

Diagonally slice 2 large bunches asparagus into 2-in. (5-cm) pieces.

Cook 1 lb (450 g) corkscrew pasta in boiling salted water until al dente, about 10 min.

Add asparagus during last 3 min.

Whisk 1/4 cup olive oil with finely grated peel of 1 lemon, 3 tbsp freshly squeezed lemon juice, 1/2 tsp dried tarragon or 3/4 tsp dried dillweed and generous pinches of salt and pepper.

Toss with drained pasta. *Serves 6 to 8.*

ASPARAGUS WITH BALSAMIC BUTTER

Boil 2 lbs (1 kg) asparagus, covered, until tender-crisp, 4 min. Heat 1 tbsp each butter and balsamic vinegar until butter melts. Toss with hot drained asparagus. Sprinkle with salt. *Serves 6 to 8.*

ASPARAGUS & RED ONION TOSS

Slice 1 lb (500 g) asparagus in half. Boil until tender-crisp, about 4 min.

Whisk 1/4 cup olive oil with 2 tbsp balsamic vinegar, finely grated peel of 1 orange and pinches of salt and pepper. Toss with hot drained asparagus and 1/4 red onion, thinly sliced.

Serve at room temperature sprinkled with grated Parmesan. *Serves 4.*

ASPARAGUS & RED ONION TOSS

B is for Broccoli . . . .

*Jalapeños and chili powder give the
classic bean salad a vibrant spicy twist in*
MEXICAN BEAN SALAD *(see recipe page 18).*

B

BEANS

Beans rank at the top of the plant protein ladder — a perfect food for these meatless times. Dress them up easily with fresh herbs and hot peppers in pastas and salads. When using canned beans, drain and rinse with cold water, unless otherwise noted. See also Green Beans.

MEXICAN BEAN SALAD

Stir 19-oz can chickpeas and
    19-oz can kidney or black beans with
    12-oz can drained corn kernels,
    2 finely chopped seeded jalapeños,
    2 chopped green peppers,
    4 chopped seeded tomatoes,
    4 sliced green onions and
    ¾ cup chopped coriander.
Whisk ¼ cup red wine vinegar with
    ¼ cup vegetable oil, 1½ tsp chili powder,
    2 tsp cumin, 1 tsp dried oregano and
    ½ tsp salt. Stir with salad. Serve right away
    or leave at room temperature up to 4 hours
    or refrigerate up to 2 days. *Serves 8 to 10.*

8-VEGETABLE RAGOUT

Sauté 1 sliced large onion, 1 sliced large carrot
    and 2 minced garlic cloves in
    1 tbsp vegetable oil for 5 min.
Stir in 1 thickly sliced celery stalk and
    2 cups thickly sliced mushrooms.
Add 19-oz can undrained Italian
    stewed tomatoes and ¼ tsp each pepper
    and hot pepper sauce. Bring to a boil.
    Cover and simmer, stirring often,
    about 20 min.
Stir in 19-oz can Romano or kidney beans
    and 1 cup corn kernels. When hot, stir in
    ¼ cup chopped fresh coriander. *Serves 6.*

FETTUCCINE WITH CHICKPEAS

Sauté 1 finely chopped leek and
    1 finely chopped celery stalk in
    2 tbsp olive oil for 2 min.
Add 28-oz can undrained diced tomatoes,
    ½ tsp hot red pepper flakes and 1 bay leaf.
    Boil gently, uncovered, stirring often, until
    thickened, about 10 min.
Cook 1 lb (450 g) fettuccine in boiling salted
    water until al dente, about 8 min.
Drain. Return to pot and add sauce and
    19-oz can chickpeas. Stir over medium
    heat until liquid is absorbed, about 2 min.
Remove bay leaf. Sprinkle with
    ½ cup grated Parmesan. *Serves 6 to 8.*

RED & GREEN BEAN SALAD

Cook 2 cups frozen green beans in boiling
    water, covered, about 1 min. Drain.
Stir with 19-oz can each red and white
    kidney beans.
Whisk ½ cup olive oil with 2 tbsp lemon juice,
    ¼ tsp dry mustard, 1 minced garlic clove,
    1 tsp granulated sugar, ¼ tsp salt and
    sprinkle with white pepper.
Stir in 2 sliced green onions and
    1 finely chopped small red onion.
Pour over beans and gently fold together.
    Serves 6 to 8.

White Bean Supper Soup

WHITE BEAN SUPPER SOUP

Sauté 1 thinly sliced onion with
 1 large minced garlic clove in
 1 tbsp olive oil until fragrant.
 Add 2 cups chicken or vegetable broth.
Stir in 19-oz can white kidney beans and
 generous pinches of pepper.
 When hot, add ½ to 1 (10-oz/300-g) bag
 torn spinach. Stir in grated Parmesan
 to taste. *Serves 2 to 3.*

SALSA & BEAN SALAD

Combine 19-oz can kidney beans or chickpeas
 with 2 thinly sliced celery stalks
 and 2 sliced green onions.
Mix ½ cup salsa with ½ tsp cumin,
 then stir in. *Serves 2 to 3.*

PASTA WITH BEANS & BASIL

Sauté 1 chopped large onion and
 3 minced large garlic cloves in
 1 tbsp olive oil, about 5 min.
Add 28-oz can undrained diced tomatoes,
 ½ cup chopped fresh basil or
 2 tsp dried basil, ½ tsp salt and
 ¼ tsp pepper. Bring to a boil.
Stir in 19-oz can kidney beans. Reduce heat
 to low and simmer, uncovered and stirring
 often, until thickened.
Toss with 1 lb (450 g) cooked penne or fusilli
 and ¼ cup grated Parmesan. *Serves 6 to 8.*

BEANS
• continued •

MEDITERRANEAN SALAD

Whisk ⅓ cup olive oil with
   2 tbsp red wine vinegar, 1 tsp Dijon,
   1 minced garlic clove and
   pinches of salt and pepper.
Add 2 (19-oz) cans white kidney beans
   or chickpeas, ½ cup thinly sliced pimento,
   1 julienned green pepper,
   ½ cup pitted black olives and
   2 tbsp capers.
Gently fold together until evenly coated.
   Serve over greens. *Serves 4 to 6.*

4-BEAN SALAD

Cook 1 lb (500 g) trimmed yellow beans
   and 12-oz (350-g) pkg frozen lima beans
   in boiling water, 2 min. Drain.
Stir with 19-oz can each red and white
   kidney beans and 1 chopped small red onion.
Whisk ½ cup vegetable oil with
   ¼ cup red wine vinegar,
   3 tbsp granulated sugar,
   4 minced garlic cloves and
   ¼ tsp each salt and cayenne.
Pour over beans and gently toss. *Serves 6 to 8.*

10-MINUTE CHILI SOUP

Stir 19-oz can undrained tomatoes with
   19-oz can undrained white kidney beans,
   1 tbsp chili powder and ¼ tsp cayenne.
Break up tomatoes with a fork. Heat, stirring
   often, over low heat, 10 min. *Serves 2 to 3.*

EASY VEGETARIAN CHILI

Drain 19-oz can kidney beans, saving liquid.
Sauté 2 minced garlic cloves and
   2 chopped onions in 1 tbsp butter or oil,
   about 5 min.
Stir in 28-oz can undrained diced tomatoes,
   2 tbsp chili powder, 1 tsp cumin,
   ½ tsp dried oregano, generous pinches
   of sugar and liquid drained from beans.
Bring mixture to a boil. Cover, reduce heat
   and simmer, 10 min. Stir in beans and just
   heat through. *Serves 4.*

BLACK BEAN & CORN SALAD

Whisk 3 tbsp olive oil with
   finely grated peel of 1 lime, ¼ cup freshly
   squeezed lime juice, 1 tsp cumin and
   ½ tsp hot red pepper flakes.
Stir in 2 (19-oz) cans black beans,
   3 cups corn kernels,
   1 coarsely chopped red pepper,
   4 thinly sliced green onions and
   ½ cup chopped fresh coriander.
Serve in scooped-out tomato halves. *Serves 8.*

CUBAN BEANS 'N' RICE WRAP

Combine 2 cups hot rice and
   1 cup canned or cooked black beans.
Divide hot filling among 3 large tortillas.
   Generously sprinkle with grated
   cheddar cheese, sliced green onions
   and chopped tomato. Roll up.
Serve with salsa or hot pepper sauce.
   Makes 3 rolls.

CURRIED SALAD

Heat ¼ cup olive oil in a frying pan. Add
2 chopped onions, 3 minced garlic cloves
and 1 tbsp minced fresh ginger. Sauté over
low heat, stirring often, 10 min.
Stir 2 (19-oz) cans chickpeas with
1 chopped unpeeled zucchini, 1 julienned
red pepper, 2 thinly sliced celery stalks
and ¼ cup chopped parsley.
Whisk 2 tbsp each olive oil and
red wine vinegar with 2 tsp each cumin
and coriander, ½ tsp turmeric and
¼ tsp each cayenne and salt.
Toss beans with hot onions and dressing.
Serves 6 to 8.

LIMA BEAN TOSS

Cook 2 (12-oz/350-g) pkgs frozen
lima beans in boiling water, about
2 min. Drain.
Combine with 1 thinly sliced small onion
and 1 julienned red pepper.
Whisk ⅓ cup olive oil with
2 tbsp red wine vinegar,
1 minced garlic clove, 2 tsp Dijon
and ⅛ tsp pepper. Toss with bean
mixture. Sprinkle with chopped parsley.
Serves 4.

LIMA BEAN TOSS

BROCCOLI

A versatile vegetable that is as good raw as it is boiled, steamed or sautéed, broccoli deserves its nutritional superstar status. Use it in salads, soups or on pizzas.

PECAN-BUTTER BROCCOLI

Break **2 heads broccoli** into florets. Cook in 2 in. (5 cm) boiling water until tender-crisp, from 3 to 4 min.
Melt ¼ **cup butter** until it begins to brown. Add ½ **cup coarsely chopped pecans** and sauté until golden brown.
Toss with drained broccoli. Season with **salt and pepper**. *Serves 8.*

BROCCOLI & MUSTARD VINAIGRETTE

Break **1 head broccoli** into florets. Cook in 1 in. (2.5 cm) boiling water until tender-crisp, 2 to 3 min.
Drain and immediately toss with **2 tbsp olive oil** whisked with 1½ **tsp Dijon** and **1 tbsp red wine vinegar**. *Serves 4 to 6.*

GREAT GARLICKY BROCCOLI

Break **1 large head broccoli** into florets. Trim and peel stalks. Slice into ½-in. (1-cm) rounds. Keep separate.
In a frying pan, heat **2 tsp olive oil** with **2 large minced garlic cloves** and ¾ **cup chicken or vegetable broth**. Add stalks and cook, uncovered, for 2 min.
Toss in florets. Stir-fry over high heat until bright green and liquid is evaporated, about 4 min. Sprinkle with ¼ **cup grated Parmesan**.
Serve topped with additional cheese or a dollop of sour cream or yogurt. *Serves 4 to 6.*

ORIENTAL STIR-FRY

Sauté **1 minced large garlic clove** in **2 tsp peanut oil** for 2 min.
Add **1 head broccoli**, cut into florets, and ¼ **cup water**. Stir-fry until tender-crisp, from 4 to 6 min. Toss with **2 to 3 tsp teriyaki sauce**. *Serves 4 to 6.*

PARMESAN-ALMOND TOSS

Break **1 head broccoli** into florets. Cook in 1 in. (2.5 cm) boiling water until tender-crisp, from 2 to 3 min.
Toss with ¼ **cup grated Parmesan** and **2 tbsp toasted slivered almonds**. *Serves 4 to 6.*

THE BIG CARROT'S BROCCOLI SALAD

Break **1 head broccoli** into florets. Cook in 1 in. (2.5 cm) boiling water until tender-crisp, from 2 to 3 min. Drain.
In a food processor, combine **3 tbsp freshly squeezed lemon juice**, **3 tbsp finely chopped fresh basil or mint**, **2 tbsp pine nuts**, **1 tsp liquid honey** and **pinch of salt**.
Then, with machine running, slowly add ⅓ **cup olive oil**.
Toss with broccoli. Sprinkle with **2 tbsp pine nuts**. *Serves 4 to 6.*

VEGGIE CAESAR PIZZA

Preheat oven to 425°F (220°C).

Pat 1 lb (500 g) pizza dough over a greased 14-in. (35-cm) pizza pan, forming a rim around edge.

Toss 3 cups mixed chopped fresh vegetables, such as broccoli, zucchini, roasted sweet peppers, seeded tomatoes and mushrooms, with
$\frac{1}{3}$ cup creamy Caesar dressing. Spread over crust.

Scatter with $\frac{1}{2}$ cup grated Parmesan and 2 cups grated mixed cheese, such as Asiago, mozzarella and cheddar.

Bake on bottom rack of preheated oven until golden, about 18 min.
Makes 1 large pizza, about 8 slices.

BROCCOLI, RED PEPPER & CHÈVRE TOSS

Break 2 heads broccoli into florets. Cook in boiling water until tender-crisp, from 3 to 4 min.

Drain and combine with 2 roasted peeled red peppers or 7$\frac{1}{2}$-oz (250-mL) jar drained roasted red peppers, cut into bite-size pieces.

Whisk 3 tbsp olive oil with
2 tbsp balsamic vinegar,
1 minced garlic clove,
$\frac{1}{4}$ tsp each salt and pepper.
Toss with vegetables.

Dot with $\frac{1}{2}$ cup crumbled creamy chèvre or feta cheese.

Sprinkle with 2 tbsp toasted sesame seeds.
Serves 8.

BROCCOLI, RED PEPPER & CHÈVRE TOSS

BROCCOLI
◆ continued ◆

GINGERED BROCCOLI

Break **2 bunches broccoli** into florets.
Peel stems, then slice diagonally into
¼-inch (0.5-cm) pieces.
Heat **2 tbsp peanut oil** with
4 thin slices fresh ginger.
Add broccoli and stir-fry, from 6 to 8 min.
Remove ginger. Season with **salt and pepper**.
Serves 8.

BROCCOLI IN NUT BUTTER

Break **I large head broccoli** into florets.
Cook in 1 in. (2.5 cm) boiling water until
tender-crisp, from 2 to 3 min.
Heat **I tbsp butter** in a large frying pan with
I minced garlic clove for 2 min.
Toss with drained broccoli and
¼ cup coarsely chopped walnuts or almonds
and stir for 2 min. *Serves 4 to 6.*

EASY FALL RICE & BROCCOLI

In a saucepan, melt **I tsp butter**. Stir in
I cup long-grain rice until coated, then
2 cups chicken or vegetable broth.
Cover and bring to a boil. Simmer,
covered, 10 min.
Stir in **2 sliced peeled carrots**. Cook for 5 min.
Stir in **1½ cups small broccoli florets**.
Continue cooking, covered, until liquid is
absorbed, about 5 to 10 more min.
Add **salt and pepper**. *Serves 2 to 3.*

ROASTED PEPPER & BROCCOLI SALAD

Break **2 large heads broccoli** into florets and
cook in boiling water until tender-crisp,
from 3 to 4 min. Drain.
Combine with **3 small peeled oranges**, sliced
into rounds, **5 thinly sliced green onions**
and **⅓ cup small black olives**.
Drain **7½-oz (250-mL) jar roasted red
peppers** and slice into strips or slice
2 roasted peeled red peppers. Set aside.
Whisk **2 tbsp olive oil** with **3 tbsp balsamic
or white wine vinegar**, **2 tsp Dijon** and
¼ tsp each salt and cayenne. Toss with
broccoli mixture.
Serve on **a bed of greens** scattered with
red peppers. *Serves 8.*

CREAMY BROCCOLI SOUP

Sauté **I chopped onion** in **2 tbsp butter** until
softened, about 5 min.
Break **2 heads broccoli** into florets and peel
and cut stalks into 2-in. (5-cm) pieces.
Add to pan with **2 cups chicken or
vegetable broth**. Cover and simmer until
softened, about 12 min.
Purée mixture in a food processor. Return
purée to saucepan. Stir in **3 cups milk** and
¼ tsp each salt and pepper. Heat through,
stirring often.
Stir in **I cup sour cream**. Serve hot or chilled.
Serves 8.

*DILLED PARTY
VEGETABLES*

GARLIC STIR-FRY

Sauté **2** minced garlic cloves in
   1 tbsp peanut or olive oil for 2 min.
Add **1** head broccoli, cut into florets, and
   ¼ cup water. Stir-fry until tender-crisp,
   about 4 to 6 min. *Serves 4 to 6.*

BROCCOLI WITH RED PEPPER

Stir-fry **1** bunch broccoli, broken into florets,
   with **3** large thin slices ginger and
   1 minced garlic clove in
   3 tbsp vegetable oil until tender-crisp,
   about 2 min.
Add **1** julienned red pepper and
   ½ cup sliced drained water chestnuts.
Stir-fry for 1 min. Remove ginger. Serve
   immediately. *Serves 8.*

DILLED PARTY VEGETABLES

Break **3** heads broccoli and **1** cauliflower into
   florets. Combine with **4** thinly sliced carrots.
   Cook in boiling salted water until
   tender-crisp, from 4 to 6 min.
Whisk **⅓** cup olive oil with **2** tbsp white
   wine vinegar, **1** tbsp each Dijon and
   granulated sugar, **¼** cup chopped fresh dill
   or **1½** tsp dried dillweed and **¾** tsp each
   salt and curry powder or paprika.
   Toss with drained vegetables.
Serve at room temperature. *Serves 12.*

C is for Carrots . . .

CORN 'N' CHEDDAR CHOWDER *(see recipe page 32)* capitalizes on everyday ingredients from corn niblets to milk. But the taste is far from ordinary, with nippy cheddar adding creamy smoothness and hot red pepper flakes an unexpected kick.

C

CABBAGE

*The cultivation of cabbage has led to a variety of strains, with leaves
ranging from crinkled to smooth, ruby red to pale green.
Cook briefly, uncovered, by sautéing or stir-frying. Either way, it's an economical move.*

CABBAGE 'N' CARROT SLAW

Mix **8 cups** shredded cabbage with
  2 coarsely grated large carrots,
  4 thinly sliced green onions and
  ½ cup chopped fresh parsley, arugula
  or coriander.
Whisk **½ cup** rice wine vinegar or
  white vinegar with **¼ cup** granulated sugar,
  2 tbsp minced fresh ginger or
  1 tsp dried ground ginger and
  ½ tsp each salt and hot red pepper flakes.
Toss with vegetables. *Serves 8 to 10.*

QUICK COLESLAW

Stir **2 cups** shredded cabbage with
  2 cups shredded spinach,
  ¼ cup store-bought coleslaw dressing
  or mayonnaise, **¼ tsp** caraway seeds and
  pinch of paprika. *Serves 2 to 4.*

AVOCADO COLESLAW

Whisk **1 tbsp** vegetable oil with
  1 tbsp freshly squeezed lemon juice,
  1 minced large garlic clove, **¾ tsp** salt
  and **¼ tsp** cayenne.
Combine **4 cups** finely shredded
  green or napa cabbage and
  3 chopped seeded large tomatoes.
  Toss with dressing. Stir in
  1 diced peeled avocado.
Serve right away or refrigerate
  up to half a day. *Serves 6 to 8.*

3-FRUIT PICNIC SLAW

Whisk **¼ cup** freshly squeezed lemon juice
  with **1 tbsp** granulated sugar,
  1 tbsp vegetable oil and **½ tsp** salt.
Stir in drained **14-oz** can crushed pineapple,
  8 cups finely shredded cabbage and
  1 thinly sliced peeled orange.
Let sit for 30 min. Stir in
  2 cups sliced strawberries.
  Serves 8 to 10.

HOT & SPICY SLAW

In a large bowl, whisk **½ cup** mayonnaise
  with **¼ cup** sour cream,
  1 minced garlic clove, **1 tsp** cumin,
  ¼ tsp each ground coriander, chili powder,
  hot red pepper flakes and salt and
  pinch of cayenne pepper.
Stir in **½** thinly sliced small green cabbage,
  1 thinly sliced red pepper and
  2 thinly sliced green onions. *Serves 4 to 6.*

NORTH AFRICAN CABBAGE SALAD

Mix **8 cups** shredded cabbage with
  2 grated carrots and **¼ cup** chopped
  fresh mint or **1 tbsp** crumbled dried mint.
Whisk **3 tbsp** olive oil with
  ¼ cup freshly squeezed lemon juice,
  1 minced small garlic clove and
  ½ tsp salt. Stir into salad.
Let stand at room temperature, about
  30 min. *Serves 8 to 10.*

CURRIED CABBAGE

Sauté 1 minced garlic clove in 2 tbsp butter.
Stir in 2 tsp each curry powder and sugar
    and ½ head shredded cabbage.
Stir-fry over medium-high heat, until
    tender-crisp, 5 min. *Serves 4.*

RED CABBAGE & ONION

Sauté 1 chopped red onion in 1 tbsp butter
    over medium heat for 2 min. Add
    5 cups julienned red cabbage and
    1 chopped unpeeled apple. Cook,
    stirring often, for 3 min.
Add ¾ cup water, ¼ cup balsamic vinegar
    and pinches of salt and pepper. Bring to
    a boil. Cover and simmer, stirring often,
    until cabbage is tender, from 10 to 15 min.
Toss with 2 tsp caraway seeds. *Serves 4 to 6.*

FRESH VEGETABLE SLAW

Mix ½ shredded red cabbage with
    1 julienned red pepper,
    1 julienned green pepper,
    2 coarsely grated carrots,
    ¼ lb (125 g) thinly sliced mushrooms,
    1 cup blanched snow peas and
    3 cups broccoli florets.
Whisk ½ cup vegetable oil with
    3 tbsp freshly squeezed lemon juice,
    3 minced garlic cloves,
    2 tbsp granulated sugar,
    2 tsp dry mustard and
    ¼ tsp each cayenne and salt.
Toss with vegetables. *Serves 6 to 8.*

FRESH VEGETABLE SLAW

ABCDEFGHIJKLMNOPQRSTUVWXYZ

CARROTS

Carrots are a naturally sweet vegetable rich in beta-carotene. Add them to everything from salads to slaws to spice bars. And don't overcook — carrots are best with a little bite.

CARROT-SPICE BARS

Preheat oven to 350°F (180°C). Grease a
   9x13-in. (3-L) baking pan.
Stir 1½ cups grated carrot with
   1 cup shredded sweetened coconut and
   ½ cup each raisins, coarsely chopped nuts
   and candied pineapple.
In a small bowl, beat 2 eggs with ¾ cup each
   brown sugar and vegetable oil.
In another bowl, stir 1 cup all-purpose flour
   with 1 tsp each baking soda and cinnamon
   and ¼ tsp each nutmeg, allspice and salt.
Pour in egg mixture. Stir just until dry
   ingredients are wet. Fold in carrot mixture.
Turn into greased baking pan. Smooth top
   and bake, from 25 to 30 min. Cool on a
   rack. *Makes 48 bars.*

SPICY MOROCCAN SALAD

Sauté 1 thinly sliced large red onion with
   1 tbsp cumin, ½ tsp each paprika and salt
   and ¼ tsp each pepper and cayenne in
   2 tbsp olive oil, about 5 min.
Add 8 to 10 julienned carrots and ½ cup water.
   Stir often on medium-high heat until
   tender-crisp and water is evaporated.
Whisk 3 tbsp freshly squeezed lemon juice
   with 2 tbsp olive oil and 1 tbsp liquid honey.
   Toss with carrots.
Sprinkle with ¼ cup chopped fresh mint.
Serve warm or at room temperature.
   Serves 4 to 6.

VEGETABLE PURÉE

Add 1½ lbs (750 g) sliced peeled carrots
   and 1 lb (500 g) sliced peeled rutabagas
   or turnips to boiling water. Cover and
   simmer until vegetables are very soft,
   about 30 min. Drain.
Purée in a food processor with ¼ cup butter,
   2 tbsp brown sugar, ¼ tsp cinnamon and
   pinches of salt and pepper.
Sprinkle with chopped fresh parsley
   or coriander. *Serves 8.*

MAPLE-LEMON CARROTS

Combine 1¼ cups water with
   1 lb (500 g) thinly sliced carrots,
   2 tbsp unsalted butter,
   1 tbsp pure maple syrup and
   ½ tsp freshly grated lemon peel.
Boil vigorously, uncovered, stirring often,
   until most of the water is evaporated,
   at least 10 min.
Add 1 to 2 tsp freshly squeezed lemon juice
   and stir until carrots are glazed, about
   2 min. *Serves 4.*

GINGER CARROTS

Melt 1 tbsp butter in a large frying pan.
   Add ½ lb (250 g) julienned carrots and
   2 tsp minced fresh ginger.
Cook, stirring often, from 5 to 7 min.
   Sprinkle with salt, pepper and
   ¼ cup chopped fresh coriander. *Serves 4.*

MICROWAVE HERBED CARROTS

Toss 4 julienned carrots with
   2 tbsp orange juice,
   2 tbsp finely chopped fresh dill
   or ½ tsp dried dillweed and
   pinches of salt and pepper.
Microwave, covered, on high, 2 min. Stir.
   Continue microwaving for 2 to 3 more
   min. *Serves 4.*

ORIENTAL CARROT SLAW

Stir 2 cups shredded or grated carrot
   with 2 tbsp peanut sauce and
   ¼ cup chopped fresh coriander.
Refrigerate at least until chilled or up
   to a day. *Serves 2 to 3.*

CURRIED VEGETABLES

Cook ½ head cauliflower, broken into florets,
   with 3 coarsely chopped onions and
   4 thinly sliced carrots in boiling water
   until tender-crisp, about 5 to 8 min.
Stir 1 cup sour cream with 1 to 2 tbsp chutney,
   ½ to 1 tsp curry powder and ¼ tsp salt.
Drain vegetables and immediately toss with
   curry sauce and serve. *Serves 6.*

ROASTED CARROTS

In a pie plate, combine 1-lb (454-g) bag
   baby carrots with ½ cup apple, orange or
   mango juice, 1 tbsp minced fresh ginger
   and pinches of salt and pepper.
Roast, uncovered, at 375°F (190°C), until
   tender, 30 min. Stir often. *Serves 4.*

ROASTED CARROTS

CORN

New varieties of corn consistently produce incredibly sweet and succulent corn on the cob. Whether fresh, canned or frozen, it can be used for a myriad of recipes, including salsas, soups, salads or pancakes.

CORN 'N' CHEDDAR CHOWDER

Sauté 1 chopped onion and
   1 chopped red pepper in 2 tbsp butter
   for 5 min.
Stirring constantly, sprinkle with
   ¼ cup all-purpose flour and
   ½ tsp dry mustard.
Stir in 2 cups chicken or vegetable broth,
   ½ tsp each paprika and salt and
   ¼ tsp each hot red pepper flakes
   and pepper. Stir constantly, until
   slightly thickened, 4 min.
Stir in 2 finely diced potatoes and
   1½ cups corn kernels. Cover and simmer,
   stirring often, until potatoes are tender,
   about 15 min.
Add 2 cups milk. When hot, stir in
   1½ cups grated old cheddar until melted.
Serve sprinkled with sliced green onions.
   Serves 6 to 8.

ELIZABETH'S CURRIED CORN

Melt 2 tbsp butter. Add 2 tbsp all-purpose flour
   and 1 tsp curry powder. Stir constantly
   over medium heat, 2 min.
Gradually stir in ¾ cup milk and whisk
   constantly until thick.
Stir in 3 cups corn kernels, 2 sliced green
   onions and pinches of salt and pepper.
   Cover and simmer, stirring often, until
   corn is hot, about 8 min. *Serves 4.*

CORN PANCAKES

Separate 2 eggs. Whisk yolks with ¾ cup milk.
In another bowl, stir 1 cup all-purpose flour
   with 2 tsp baking powder and ½ tsp salt.
   Gradually stir in milk mixture and
   2 cups corn kernels.
Beat 2 egg whites until soft peaks form when
   beaters are lifted. Fold into flour mixture.
For each pancake, spoon ½ cup mixture onto
   a hot greased frying pan.
Cook, until golden, from 4 to 5 min. per side.
   Makes 6 pancakes.

CREAMY CURRIED CORN SALAD

Cut raw kernels from 4 ears of corn.
   Heat 2 tbsp olive oil with corn kernels,
   1 sliced red pepper, 1 minced garlic clove
   and 1 tbsp curry powder. Cook, stirring
   often, 3 min.
Stir in 1 tbsp cider vinegar, 3 tbsp water and
   2 sliced zucchini. Cover and cook until
   corn is tender, 3 more min.
Stir vegetables with 4 thinly sliced green onions,
   ¼ cup each mayonnaise and sour cream
   and ¼ tsp each salt and pepper. Toss and
   serve hot or cold. *Serves 4 to 6.*

JALAPEÑO CAJUN CORN CHILI

Sauté 1 chopped onion and 2 finely chopped
seeded jalapeños in 1 tbsp butter until
onion has softened, about 5 min.
Stir in 6 cups corn kernels, 1 tsp cumin,
½ tsp each chili powder, garlic powder,
dried leaf thyme and salt and
¼ tsp hot red pepper flakes.
Stir often for 5 to 8 min.
Add 4 coarsely chopped seeded large
tomatoes and 19-oz can drained kidney
or black beans. Stir until hot. Sprinkle
with ½ cup chopped fresh coriander.
Serves 6 to 8.

QUICK CORN SAUTÉ

Sauté 3 cups corn kernels, 1 chopped red
pepper, 3 thinly sliced green onions,
1 tsp dried oregano and pinches of salt
and pepper in 1 tbsp butter.
Stir often until corn is hot, about 5 min.
Serves 6.

SALSA CORN SALAD

Combine 4 cups corn kernels with
4 chopped seeded tomatoes,
1 chopped green pepper and
4 sliced green onions.
Whisk ¼ cup vegetable oil with
2 to 3 tbsp freshly squeezed lime juice,
4.5-oz (127-mL) can diced green chilies,
3 minced garlic cloves,
¼ tsp hot pepper sauce and
pinches of cayenne, salt and pepper.
Stir into vegetables. Sprinkle with
½ cup chopped fresh coriander.
Serves 8.

Quick
Corn Sauté

CORNMEAL

Depending on the corn it's ground from, cornmeal can be white, yellow or blue.
Use it to make fiery jalapeño-flecked muffins, easy corn bread
or cornmeal porridge, better known by its Italian name, polenta.

SIZZLING LOUISIANA CORN MUFFINS

Preheat oven to 400°F (200°C). Stir
  1 cup cornmeal with 1¼ cups buttermilk
  and ¼ tsp hot pepper sauce.
In another bowl, stir 1¼ cups all-purpose flour
  with 1½ tsp baking powder,
  1 tsp baking soda, ½ tsp salt and
  ⅓ cup granulated sugar.
Whisk 1 egg with ⅓ cup melted butter.
  Stir in cornmeal mixture. Pour into
  flour mixture. Stir just until moist.
  Stir in ⅔ cup corn kernels and
  2 tbsp snipped chives. Don't overmix.
Spoon into 12 greased muffin cups.
  Bake until golden, from 13 to 15 min.
  Makes 12 muffins.

CHEDDAR CORN BREAD

Preheat oven to 350°F (180°C). Beat
  ½ cup room-temperature butter with
  ¼ cup granulated sugar and 1 egg.
  Gradually beat in 1½ cups milk.
In another bowl, stir 1 cup each
  all-purpose flour and cornmeal
  with ½ cup grated old cheddar,
  2½ tsp baking powder and ½ tsp salt. Add
  milk mixture and stir just until blended.
Turn into a greased 8-in. (2-L) square
  baking dish. Bake until corn bread springs
  back when touched, from 35 to 40 min.
  Makes 16 squares.

SOUTHERN CORN BREAD SQUARES

Preheat oven to 425°F (220°C). Stir
  1 cup each cornmeal and all-purpose flour
  with 2 tbsp granulated sugar,
  1 tsp each baking soda and baking powder
  and ¾ tsp salt. Add 3 tbsp butter and
  cut in until mixture is crumbly.
Whisk 1 egg with 1½ cups buttermilk.
  Pour into flour mixture. Stir just until
  combined. Don't overmix.
Turn into a greased 8-in. (2-L) square
  baking dish. Bake until corn bread springs
  back when touched, from 15 to 20 min.
  Makes 16 squares.

PEPPERED MINI CORN BREAD

Preheat oven to 400°F (200°C). Stir
  1 cup each all-purpose flour and cornmeal
  with 3 tbsp granulated sugar,
  1 tbsp baking powder and ¼ tsp salt.
Whisk 1 egg with 1¼ cups milk and
  ⅓ cup melted butter. Pour into flour
  mixture.
Add ½ cup finely chopped red and green
  peppers. Stir just until combined. Don't
  overmix.
Spoon mixture into 9 (3x1-in./7.5x2.5-cm)
  greased mini loaf pans or 12 muffin
  cups. Bake until golden around edges,
  from 15 to 18 min.
  Makes 9 mini loaves or 12 muffins.

PIZZA POLENTA

Preheat oven to 400°F (200°C). Bring
1½ cups milk, 1 tbsp butter and ¼ tsp salt
to a boil. Whisk in 1 cup cornmeal and
¼ cup grated Parmesan. Reduce heat
to medium-low. Stir constantly, until
cornmeal thickens and pulls away from
sides of pan, about 3 min.

Spoon polenta into a 9-in. (23-cm) pie
plate or baking pan. Spread with
1 cup pizza sauce. Scatter with
1 thinly sliced regular or **veggie pepperoni**
and ¾ cup grated Fontina or mozzarella.
Bake on bottom rack of oven until
edge is lightly browned, about 18 min.
Serves 4 to 6.

SUSAN'S SUPPER PANCAKES

Stir 1 cup cornmeal with
¼ cup all-purpose flour,
1½ tsp baking powder,
1 tsp granulated sugar,
½ tsp each salt and baking soda.

Whisk **3 eggs** with 1½ cups buttermilk
and **2 tbsp** melted butter. Pour into
flour mixture. Stir just until smooth.
Don't overmix.

Pour a ¼-cup measure of batter onto a lightly
oiled hot frying pan. Cook until underside
is golden, about 2 min. per side. Keep
warm, while continuing to make more.

Top pancakes with **tomato salsa**.
Makes 14 pancakes.

SUSAN'S SUPPER PANCAKES

COUSCOUS

Couscous, a pale yellow granular pasta, is a mainstay of Moroccan cuisine. The instant variety that's popular in North America involves merely stirring into hot stock or water and leaving for 5 minutes to form an exotic base for your favorite vegetables.

COUSCOUS WITH SPRING VEGETABLES

Bring 1¼ cups water and ¼ tsp salt to a boil. Remove from heat. Stir in 1 cup couscous and ¼ cup raisins or currants. Cover and let stand, about 5 min.

Stir-fry 2 minced large garlic cloves, 3 cups sliced mixed vegetables, such as broccoli, peppers, celery and zucchini, in 1 tbsp olive oil, from 2 to 4 min. Sprinkle with ½ tsp paprika and pinch of cayenne and stir to coat vegetables.

Stir in 2 tbsp freshly squeezed lemon juice and 2 thinly sliced green onions. Fluff couscous and serve vegetables over top. *Serves 2 to 3.*

ALMOND-RAISIN COUSCOUS

Combine 2½ cups chicken or vegetable broth with 3 tbsp butter, ¼ cup raisins, ¼ tsp each celery salt, chili powder and pepper in a saucepan. Cover and bring to a boil. Remove from heat.

Stir in 2 cups couscous and ¼ cup coarsely chopped almonds. Cover and let stand, about 5 min.

Sprinkle with ¼ cup chopped fresh parsley. *Serves 8.*

COUSCOUS SALAD & TOMATOES

Bring 1¼ cups chicken or vegetable broth to a boil. Remove from heat. Stir in 1 cup couscous and 1 tbsp olive oil. Cover and let stand, about 5 min. Then fluff with a fork. Refrigerate, uncovered, until cool.

Whisk 2 tbsp olive oil with 2 tbsp lime or lemon juice and ¼ tsp salt.

Stir in 4 chopped seeded tomatoes. Stir into couscous with ½ cup finely chopped fresh mint. *Serves 4.*

MICROWAVE CUMIN COUSCOUS & SQUASH

Pierce 1 large acorn or small butternut squash in two places. Microwave, on high, 2 min. Cut in half. Peel and seed. Cut into 1-in. (2.5-cm) pieces.

Stir with 1½ cups water, 1 tsp butter, 1 tsp cumin or ½ tsp curry powder, ¼ tsp cinnamon and ½ tsp salt. Microwave, covered, on high, until tender, about 12 min.

Stir in 1 cup couscous and 4 sliced green onions. Cover and let stand, about 5 min. *Serves 4.*

Vegetable Couscous

SAFFRON COUSCOUS

Bring 2 cups water, 1 tbsp butter,
   1 chicken or vegetable bouillon cube and
   ¼ tsp saffron to a boil. Remove from heat.
Stir in 1½ cups couscous. Cover and let
   stand, about 5 min. Scatter with
   ½ cup slivered toasted almonds. *Serves 4.*

COUSCOUS 'N' LENTILS

Boil 1 cup water. Stir in 1 cup couscous,
   1 tbsp butter and ½ tsp salt. Cover
   and let stand, about 5 min. Then fluff.
Stir in 19-oz can rinsed drained lentils,
   3 thinly sliced green onions and
   ½ cup chopped fresh coriander or
   ¼ cup snipped fresh chives. *Serves 3 to 4.*

VEGETABLE COUSCOUS

Bring 1¼ cups water and ¼ tsp salt to a boil.
   Remove from heat. Stir in 1 cup couscous.
   Cover and let stand, about 5 min.
Combine ¼ sliced English cucumber with
   2 chopped seeded ripe tomatoes,
   4 thinly sliced green onions, ¼ cup each
   finely chopped fresh mint and fresh basil.
Whisk 2 tbsp olive oil with 3 tbsp freshly
   squeezed lemon juice. Stir into cooked
   couscous along with vegetables. *Serves 4.*

E is for Eggplants . . .

Eggplants and other fresh vegetables crown a
store-bought crust for this fast and light
MEDITERRANEAN VEGETABLE PIZZA (see recipe page 40).

EGGPLANTS

The eggplant's unique texture makes it the "steak" of vegetarians.
Slender Asian and Italian globe varieties are the mildest and sweetest.

MEDITERRANEAN VEGETABLE PIZZA

Preheat oven to 425°F (220°C). Pat
1 lb (500 g) pizza dough over a greased
14-in. (35-cm) pizza pan, forming a rim
around edge.

Sauté 1 minced garlic clove and 3 cups thinly
sliced vegetables, such as eggplant, onions,
peppers, mushrooms and zucchini, in
1 tbsp olive oil. Stir often until vegetables
are partially cooked, from 3 to 5 min.

Stir in 7½-oz can tomato sauce or
1 cup spaghetti sauce, ¾ tsp dried oregano,
½ tsp dried basil and ¼ to ½ tsp hot red
pepper flakes.

Spread over crust and sprinkle with 1 cup
grated mozzarella, ½ cup grated Asiago or
Parmesan. Dot with ½ cup goat cheese.

Bake immediately on bottom rack of
oven until golden, from 15 to 20 min.
Makes 8 wedges.

EASY-BAKE RATATOUILLE

Preheat oven to 375°F (190°C). Stir
1 finely chopped small onion with
3 minced garlic cloves, 2 cups cubed
peeled eggplant, 3 cups coarsely
chopped tomatoes with juice, 2 chopped
large green peppers, 1 tbsp capers,
2 tsp each dried basil and oregano,
1 tsp granulated sugar and ¾ tsp salt.

Place in a 9x13-in. (3-L) dish. Bake,
uncovered, in preheated oven, stirring
often, 45 min. *Serves 3 to 4.*

MOROCCAN GRILLED EGGPLANT DIP

Stir 2 tbsp olive oil with 2 minced garlic
cloves. Brush over 2 small unpeeled
Japanese eggplants, sliced lengthwise,
1 sliced small red onion and 4 sliced
plum tomatoes. Barbecue or grill, turning
occasionally, until softened and slightly
charred, from 15 to 20 min.

Purée in a food processor. Stir in
3 tbsp freshly squeezed lemon juice,
¼ cup chopped fresh coriander,
1 tsp cumin and ½ tsp salt.

Covered and refrigerated, dip will keep well
for up to 3 days.

Serve at room temperature. *Makes 3½ cups.*

RACY RATATOUILLE

Slice 1 unpeeled small eggplant, 1 onion
and 1 red pepper into 1-in. (2.5-cm) cubes.
Slice 1 zucchini into ½-in. (1-cm) slices.

Sauté onion and 2 minced garlic cloves in
1 tbsp olive oil for 5 min.

Stir in eggplant, pepper, zucchini and
8 chopped large ripe tomatoes,
¼ cup chopped fresh basil or
1 tsp dried basil, ½ tsp dried leaf thyme,
⅓ tsp salt and ¼ tsp pepper. Cook,
covered, stirring occasionally, about
30 min. *Serves 4 to 6.*

BRUSCHETTA-TOPPED SLICES

Preheat oven to 350°F (180°C). Slice
1 unpeeled eggplant, lengthwise, into
1-in. (2.5-cm) slices. Bake, covered, in
a lightly oiled baking dish for 10 min.

Combine 3 finely chopped tomatoes with
3 minced garlic cloves, 3 thinly sliced
green onions, 1 tbsp chopped fresh basil
or ½ tsp dried basil, 2 tbsp olive oil and
¼ tsp each salt and pepper. Scatter tomato
mixture over eggplant. Sprinkle with
¼ cup grated Parmesan.

Bake, uncovered, until cheese is golden, from
15 to 25 more min. *Serves 6.*

EGGPLANT STEAKS WITH CHÈVRE & TOMATOES

Preheat barbecue and oil grill. Slice
2 large eggplants, lengthwise, into
8 (½-in./1-cm) thick slices.

Whisk 2 tbsp freshly squeezed lemon juice
with ¼ cup olive oil, 1 tbsp granulated sugar,
2 tbsp finely chopped fresh basil, ¼ tsp dried
oregano, ½ tsp salt and 2 minced large garlic
cloves. Brush over both sides of eggplant.
Barbecue until grill marks appear on
undersides, about 4 min. Brush and turn.

Dot with ½ cup creamy chèvre. Continue
barbecuing until grill marks appear on
undersides, about 3 min.

Top 4 eggplant slices with 2 sliced tomatoes
and 12 basil leaves. Top with remaining
eggplant, cheese-side down.
Makes 4 double-decker steaks.

EGGPLANT STEAKS WITH CHÈVRE & TOMATOES

G is for Greens . . .

Fresh juicy peaches combine with green onions, coriander and a lemon vinaigrette to add jazz in WILD RICE & PEACH SALAD (see recipe page 44).

GRAINS

Try quick-cooking bulgur, quinoa, millet and oats for a variety of high-fibre dishes.
Everything from pancakes to salads can quickly grace the breakfast or dinner table.
See also Cornmeal, Couscous and Rice.

WILD RICE & PEACH SALAD

Bring 1 cup wild rice, 3 cups water and
    1 tsp salt to a boil. Cover and simmer
    until rice is tender, about 50 min. Drain.
Whisk 2 tbsp olive oil with 1 to 2 tbsp freshly
    squeezed lemon or lime juice, 1 minced
    garlic clove and ½ tsp salt. Stir into hot
    rice. Refrigerate, uncovered, until cool.
Stir in 2 chopped ripe peaches or nectarines
    or 1 ripe mango, 3 thinly sliced green onions
    and ½ cup chopped fresh coriander.
Serve on a bed of greens. *Serves 4 to 6.*

TEXAS BARLEY SALAD

Bring 1 cup pearl barley and 3 cups chicken
    or vegetable bouillon or water to a boil.
    Cover and simmer until barley is cooked
    al dente, about 25 min. Stir occasionally.
    Drain and cool.
Whisk ⅓ cup vegetable oil with
    2 tbsp white vinegar, 2 minced garlic cloves,
    1 to 2 tsp cumin and ½ tsp chili powder.
Add 3 thinly sliced green onions, 2 chopped
    tomatoes and 1½ cups drained corn
    kernels. Fold in barley and ⅓ cup finely
    chopped parsley. *Serves 4 to 6.*

GREEK BARLEY SALAD

Bring 1 cup pearl barley and 3 cups chicken
    or vegetable bouillon or water to a boil.
    Cover and simmer until barley is cooked
    al dente, about 25 min. Stir occasionally.
    Drain and cool.
Combine 1 julienned red pepper with
    ½ chopped unpeeled English cucumber,
    1 thinly sliced green onion, 1 chopped
    large tomato, ½ cup black olives and
    4 cups torn romaine lettuce.
Whisk ⅓ cup olive oil with 3 tbsp freshly
    squeezed lemon juice, 2 minced garlic
    cloves, ½ tsp dried oregano, ¼ tsp salt
    and pinches of pepper. Stir with barley
    and vegetables.
Sprinkle with ½ cup crumbled feta. *Serves 6.*

TRIPLE-HERBED TABBOULEH

Soak 1 cup bulgur in boiling water,
    10 minutes. Drain well.
Whisk 1 tbsp olive oil with
    3 to 4 tbsp freshly squeezed lemon juice,
    1 tsp each sugar and salt and
    dash of hot pepper sauce.
Stir into bulgur with 3 chopped seeded
    tomatoes and ¼ cup each chopped
    fresh parsley, mint and green onions.
Serve right away or refrigerate, covered,
    up to 2 days. *Serves 4.*

*MOROCCAN
RICE 'N' CHICKPEA
SALAD*

QUINOA TABBOULEH SALAD

Bring 1¾ cups water to a boil. Stir in
  1 cup well-rinsed quinoa and
  pinches of salt. Cover and simmer
  until water is absorbed and quinoa
  grains are transparent, about 15 min.
Whisk ½ cup olive oil with ¼ cup freshly
  squeezed lemon juice, ½ tsp salt and
  ¼ tsp chili powder. Stir in hot quinoa.
  Cool to room temperature.
Chop ¼ English cucumber, 2 tomatoes,
  1 green pepper, 5 green onions and
  1 large bunch parsley. Toss with quinoa.
Refrigerate for at least 1 hour. *Serves 8.*

MOROCCAN RICE 'N' CHICKPEA SALAD

Cook 1 cup wild-and-white-rice blend
  according to package directions. Drain.
Stir ¼ cup tahini with
  finely grated peel of ½ lemon,
  1 minced large garlic clove,
  1½ tsp olive oil, ½ tsp salt and
  generous pinch of cayenne.
Stir in 2 tbsp freshly squeezed lemon juice
  and 2 tbsp water to make a thick
  pourable dressing.
Stir into rice with 19-oz can drained chickpeas,
  2 grated carrots, 3 sliced green onions and
  ½ cup chopped fresh parsley or coriander.
  Serves 8.

GRAINS
• *continued* •

WILD RICE CITRUS SALAD

Cook 1½ cups long-grain rice and
  1½ cups wild rice separately according
  to package directions.
Toss with 3 sliced green onions,
  1 chopped red pepper and 3 oranges,
  peeled and sliced.
Whisk ½ cup vegetable oil with juice of
  1 lemon and pinches of salt and pepper.
Toss with rice mixture. *Serves 10 to 12.*

MILLET & FETA SALAD

Cook 1 cup whole millet and generous
  pinches of salt in boiling water until
  tender, 20 minutes. Drain and cool.
Add ¼ finely chopped English cucumber,
  1 finely chopped celery stalk, 1 chopped
  red pepper, 1 sliced green onion and
  ½ cup crumbled feta.
Whisk 2 tbsp freshly squeezed lemon juice
  with 1 tbsp olive oil and pinch of cayenne
  and stir in. *Serves 4.*

OATMEAL BREAKFAST BONANZA

Bring 1½ cups water and ¼ tsp salt to a boil.
  Stir in ⅔ cup quick-cooking rolled oats,
  ¼ cup raisins and 1 snipped dried apricot.
  Stir often for 2 to 3 min. Cover, remove
  from heat and let stand for a few minutes.
Sprinkle with cinnamon and brown sugar
  and serve with milk. *Serves 1.*

WHOLE-GRAIN PANCAKES

Stir ½ cup each whole-wheat flour and
  all-purpose flour with ½ cup oat bran,
  1 tsp baking powder, ½ tsp each baking
  soda and salt and 3 tbsp brown sugar.
Whisk 2 eggs with 2¼ cups buttermilk and
  ⅓ cup melted butter. Pour into flour
  mixture. Stir just until dry ingredients
  are moist. Let stand for 10 min.
In a greased frying pan, pour ⅓ cup batter.
  Cook until underside is golden, about
  2 min. per side. Repeat with remaining
  batter. *Makes 12 pancakes.*

BRAN & RAISIN PANCAKES

Combine 2 cups bran cereal with
  1½ cups whole-wheat flour,
  1 tbsp brown sugar and ½ tsp salt.
Whisk 2 eggs with 3 cups milk. Stir in
  ¼ cup melted butter and ½ cup raisins.
  Pour into flour mixture. Stir just until
  moistened. Let stand for 10 min.
In a hot greased frying pan, pour ⅓ cup
  batter. Cook until underside is golden,
  about 2 min. per side. Repeat with
  remaining batter.
Serve with yogurt and fresh fruit.
  Makes 14 pancakes.

OAT & RAISIN COOKIES

Preheat oven to 325°F (160°C). Stir
  1 cup each whole-wheat flour and
  all-purpose flour with 1 tsp each baking
  soda and salt and ½ tsp cinnamon.
Beat 1½ cups room-temperature butter with
  1¾ cups firmly packed brown sugar. Beat
  in 2 eggs, 2 tbsp milk and 1½ tsp vanilla.
  Gradually stir in flour mixture until mixed.
Stir in 3 cups rolled oats (not instant),
  1 cup raisins and 1 cup chopped nuts.
Spoon heaping tablespoons onto a greased
  baking sheet, 5 in. (12 cm) apart. Press down
  with wet tines of a fork to ¼ in. (0.5 cm)
  thickness. Bake until edges are golden,
  from 10 to 12 min. *Makes 4 dozen cookies.*

QUICK BRAN MUFFINS

Preheat oven to 400°F (200°C). Combine
  1 cup all-purpose flour with
  2 tsp baking powder, ½ tsp salt,
  ¼ tsp cinnamon and 3 tbsp brown sugar.
  Stir in 1¼ cups natural bran.
Whisk 1 egg with 1 cup milk,
  ¼ cup vegetable oil and 2 tbsp molasses.
Pour into flour mixture with ½ cup raisins.
  Stir just until moistened. Spoon into
  12 greased muffin cups. Bake until golden,
  from 18 to 20 min. *Makes 12 muffins.*

KASHA WITH FRUIT

Sauté 1 chopped large onion with 2 minced
  garlic cloves in 2 tbsp butter or olive oil,
  5 min. Add 1 cup whole kasha and stir
  constantly until coated with butter.
Stir in 2 cups water and ½ tsp salt and bring
  to a boil. Cover and simmer until kasha
  is tender and liquid is absorbed, about
  10 min.
Whisk ⅓ cup olive oil with 2 tbsp freshly
  squeezed lemon juice, 2 tsp Dijon and
  2 tsp brown sugar. Stir in hot kasha. Cool.
Add 1½ cups chopped nectarines or
  peaches, 1 chopped green pepper
  and ½ cup chopped coriander.
  Serves 4 to 6.

Quick Bran Muffins

GREEN BEANS

Whether you gravitate to pencil-thin haricots verts or broader larger beans with bulging seeds, green beans are soft in taste. The texture, though, depends on when they were picked and can range from al dente to stringy.

STIR-FRIED GARLIC BEANS

Sauté 1 minced garlic clove in ½ tbsp each vegetable oil and butter for 2 min.
Add 1 lb (500 g) trimmed green beans, 1 chopped red pepper and ½ cup water.
Sauté, stirring often, until tender-crisp, about 8 min. Toss with generous pinches of salt and pepper. Drain and place on a platter.
Add 1 tsp vegetable oil to pan and ¼ cup coarsely chopped almonds, peanuts or cashews. Stir until golden, from 2 to 3 min. Scatter over beans. *Serves 4.*

GLAZED BALSAMIC BEANS

In a large frying pan, cook ½ lb (250 g) trimmed green beans in boiling water for 2 min. Drain.
Add 2 tbsp balsamic or red wine vinegar, 1 tbsp brown sugar, 1 tbsp butter and pinches of salt and pepper. Stir until glazed, about 2 min. *Serves 2.*

TARRAGON BEAN & RED ONION SALAD

Cook 2 lbs (1 kg) trimmed green beans in boiling water until tender-crisp, about 3 min. Drain. Combine with 1 chopped small red onion and 2 thinly sliced celery stalks.
Whisk ½ cup vegetable oil with ⅓ cup tarragon vinegar or freshly squeezed lemon juice, 2 minced garlic cloves and pinches of salt, pepper and sugar.
Toss with bean mixture. *Serves 8.*

FRESH BASIL & BEAN SALAD

Cook ¾ lb (375 g) each trimmed yellow and green beans in boiling water until tender-crisp, about 3 min. Drain.
Combine with 3 chopped seeded large tomatoes and 1 cup black olives.
Whisk ½ cup vegetable oil with 3 tbsp freshly squeezed lemon juice, 3 minced garlic cloves, 1 tsp granulated sugar, pinches of salt and pepper and ⅓ cup finely chopped fresh basil.
Toss with bean mixture. *Serves 8.*

BEAN & PEPPER SAUTÉ

Sauté 2 minced garlic cloves in 3 tbsp olive oil, 2 min. Add 2 lbs (1 kg) trimmed green beans and sauté for 3 min.
Add 2 julienned yellow peppers, 1½ tsp dried marjoram and finely grated peel of 1 lemon. Sauté until peppers are cooked, about 3 more min.
Sprinkle with 2 tbsp freshly squeezed lemon juice and pinches of salt and pepper. *Serves 8.*

GREEN BEANS WITH HAZELNUTS

Cook 2 lbs (1 kg) trimmed green beans in boiling water until tender-crisp, 3 to 5 min. Drain.
Heat 2 tbsp butter with ¾ cup coarsely chopped hazelnuts until golden, about 2 min. Pour over beans. Sprinkle with salt and white pepper. *Serves 8.*

CASHEWS WITH BUTTERED GREEN BEANS

Cook 2 lbs (1 kg) trimmed green
   or yellow beans in boiling water
   until tender-crisp, 3 min. Drain.
Melt 2 tbsp butter in a small
   frying pan. When bubbly, stir in
   1 minced garlic clove and cook,
   stirring often, until hot and fragrant,
   about 1 min.
Toss with beans and ¼ cup chopped
   fresh basil or coriander and
   generous pinches of salt and pepper.
Sprinkle with ½ cup coarsely chopped
   toasted cashews. *Serves 8.*

HARLEQUIN BEANS WITH TOASTED PECANS

Cook 1 lb (500 g) each trimmed
   green and yellow beans and
   2 julienned red and orange peppers
   in boiling water, covered, until
   tender-crisp, from 4 to 7 min. Drain.
Heat 1 tbsp butter with
   ¼ cup chopped pecans or slivered
   almonds. Stir-fry until golden,
   from 2 to 3 min.
Pour over vegetables. Sprinkle with
   pinches of salt and pepper. *Serves 8.*

HARLEQUIN BEANS WITH TOASTED PECANS

GREENS

*A garden salad composed of several different kinds of greens, from Bibb
to radicchio, and drizzled with either a simple vinaigrette or a fancy sherry dressing,
can begin or end any meal with style.*

WATERCRESS & ROMAINE SALAD

Tear 2 heads romaine and 1 bunch watercress
into bite-size pieces. Combine with
1 sliced English cucumber,
2 thinly sliced green onions or
¼ cup snipped fresh chives.
Whisk ½ cup olive or peanut oil with
3 tbsp red wine vinegar, 2 to 3 tsp Dijon,
2 minced garlic cloves and
generous pinches of salt, pepper and sugar.
Toss with salad. *Serves 10.*

BALSAMIC GREENS

Toss 10 cups mixed lettuce greens, such as
Boston, romaine, Bibb or radicchio, torn
into bite-size pieces, until combined.
Whisk 2 tbsp balsamic vinegar with
2 tbsp olive oil, 2 tbsp finely chopped
fresh basil and pinches of salt and pepper.
Drizzle over salad and toss. *Serves 4 to 6.*

RADICCHIO SALAD

Combine 1 head torn Bibb lettuce and
¼ to ½ head torn radicchio.
Add 1 julienned yellow pepper.
Whisk ⅓ cup olive oil with 1½ tsp Dijon,
2 tbsp balsamic or red wine vinegar
and pinches of salt, pepper and sugar.
Toss with salad. *Serves 4 to 6.*

GREEN & RED TOSSED SALAD

Whisk 2 tbsp balsamic vinegar with
1 tsp Dijon, 1 minced large garlic clove,
generous pinches of hot red pepper flakes,
dried basil, oregano, salt, pepper and sugar.
Gradually drizzle in ⅓ cup olive oil,
whisking constantly.
Combine 1 head each red-tipped leaf lettuce,
radicchio and Boston lettuce and
1 Belgian endive, broken into
bite-size pieces.
Drizzle dressing over salad and toss. *Serves 8.*

MIXED GREENS WITH MAPLE VINAIGRETTE

Whisk ¼ cup olive or vegetable oil
with 2 tbsp maple syrup,
2 tbsp freshly squeezed lemon juice,
½ tsp Dijon, ¼ tsp salt and
pinch of pepper.
Taste and stir in 1 more tbsp lemon juice
and ¼ tsp tarragon (optional).
Toss with 12 cups bite-size pieces mixed
salad greens or spinach.
Sprinkle with ¼ cup coarsely chopped
toasted hazelnuts, pecans or walnuts.
Serve right away. *Serves 6 to 8.*

TEX-MEX TOMATO SALAD

Stir $\frac{1}{3}$ cup mayonnaise with
2 minced garlic cloves and
$\frac{1}{2}$ tsp each chili powder and cumin.
Stir in 4 coarsely chopped large tomatoes.
Combine I small head romaine,
cut into bite-size pieces, and
4 thinly sliced green onions.
Add tomato mixture and toss.
Stir in I cup grated Monterey Jack
or mozzarella. Sprinkle with
2 cups bite-size pieces of corn chips.
Serves 6 to 8.

WARM SHERRY SALAD

Heat $\frac{1}{2}$ cup orange juice with $\frac{1}{4}$ cup sherry,
I tbsp Dijon, I minced garlic clove and
$\frac{1}{4}$ tsp each salt and sugar.
Boil gently, whisking often, until reduced to
less than half a cup. Remove from heat.
Slowly whisk in $\frac{1}{4}$ cup olive oil.
Pour warm dressing over 16 cups bite-size
pieces mixed salad greens and toss.
Serves 8 to 10.

THYME PECAN SALAD

Combine I small head romaine and
$\frac{1}{2}$ bunch arugula or watercress, broken
into bite-size pieces.
Whisk $\frac{1}{4}$ cup olive oil with
I to 2 tbsp freshly squeezed lemon juice,
I tbsp Dijon and $\frac{1}{2}$ tsp dried leaf thyme.
Toss with salad.
Sprinkle with $\frac{1}{4}$ cup toasted pecans. *Serves 4.*

LIME-HONEY STRAWBERRY SALAD

Mix I small head each red-tipped leaf lettuce,
Boston lettuce and curly endive or
bunch of arugula, torn into bite-size
pieces, about 8 cups.
Add 2 cups sliced strawberries.
Whisk $\frac{1}{2}$ cup light sour cream
with I tbsp liquid honey,
$\frac{1}{2}$ tsp finely grated lime peel and
$\frac{1}{4}$ tsp each salt and pepper.
Pour over greens and toss gently. *Serves 4 to 6.*

Warm Sherry Salad

GREENS
• continued •

PEAR & HONEY-MUSTARD SALAD

Whisk 1 tbsp olive oil with
  1 tbsp freshly squeezed lemon juice,
  1 tsp liquid honey and ½ tsp grainy mustard.
Toss with 2 sliced pears and
  4 to 6 cups mixed salad greens. *Serves 4.*

WALNUT GREENS

Whisk ¼ cup walnut or olive oil
  with 1 tbsp white wine vinegar,
  1 tsp grainy Dijon,
  ¼ tsp each salt and pepper.
Combine 1 head each radicchio and
  Boston lettuce, torn into bite-size
  pieces, with 2 sliced green onions.
  Toss with dressing.
Sprinkle with ¼ cup coarsely chopped
  toasted walnuts. *Serves 4 to 6.*

WARM SOPHISTICATED SALAD

Sauté 4 cups sliced mushrooms in
  2 tbsp olive oil over medium-high heat
  until just lightly browned, about 10 min.
Whisk 1 tbsp white wine vinegar with
  ½ tsp Dijon and pinches of salt and pepper.
Stir into mushrooms and remove from heat.
Toss with 4 to 6 cups mixed lettuce greens.
Sprinkle with ¼ cup crumbled blue or
  feta cheese. *Serves 4 to 6.*

TARRAGON TOMATO SALAD

Cover a serving platter with 4 cups mixed
  salad greens. Arrange 8 sliced yellow,
  orange or red small tomatoes over top.
  Sprinkle with pinches of salt and sugar.
Whisk 3 tbsp olive oil with 2 tbsp white or
  white wine vinegar, 2 tsp honey mustard,
  2 tsp chopped fresh tarragon or
  ¼ tsp dried tarragon and ¼ tsp salt.
Drizzle over tomatoes. *Serves 4 to 6.*

GREENS WITH ROQUEFORT VINAIGRETTE

Whisk ⅓ cup olive oil with
  1 tbsp freshly squeezed lemon juice,
  2 tbsp finely crumbled Roquefort and
  pinches of salt and pepper.
Toss with 8 to 10 cups mixed garden greens,
  such as romaine, Bibb or leafy lettuce or
  spinach. *Serves 6.*

TOSSED SALAD WITH FRESH HERB DRESSING

Whisk ½ cup olive oil with
  3 tbsp white vinegar, 1 tsp Dijon,
  1 tbsp each chopped fresh or
  ½ tsp each dried chervil, tarragon and
  basil, pinches of salt, pepper and sugar
  and 1 minced garlic clove.
Combine 1 head torn romaine lettuce,
  ½ lb (250 g) thinly sliced mushrooms,
  2 diced tomatoes and 1 sliced red onion.
  Toss with dressing. *Serves 6.*

*GARDEN
SALAD
WITH PITA
CROUTONS*

RITA'S SPAGHETTINI WITH GREENS

Prepare 15 torn large escarole leaves, 8 torn
large romaine leaves, 2 chopped onions,
1/2 finely chopped small fennel bulb,
2 minced garlic cloves and 1 fresh or dried
whole hot pepper.

Cook 1/2 lb (225 g) spaghettini in boiling
salted water until al dente, about 8 min.

Meanwhile, cook vegetables in 2 tbsp olive oil,
covered and stirring often, for 10 min.

Toss with drained pasta. Add 1/2 cup grated
Parmesan, 1/2 tsp pepper and 1/4 tsp salt.
Remove hot pepper. *Serves 4.*

GARDEN SALAD WITH PITA CROUTONS

Brush 3 rounds pita with 2 tbsp olive oil
mixed with 2 minced garlic cloves. Cut into
1-in. (2.5-cm) pieces. Toast on a baking
sheet at 375°F (190°C), from 12 to 15 min.

Stir 3 chopped seeded tomatoes with
1/2 cup each chopped parsley and fresh mint,
3 thinly sliced green onions, 1/4 cup
chopped red onion, 1/2 chopped peeled
cucumber and 1 chopped green pepper.

Whisk 1/3 cup freshly squeezed lemon juice
with 2 minced large garlic cloves,
3/4 tsp salt and 1/4 tsp pepper.
Gradually whisk in 1/3 cup olive oil.

Toss with tomato mixture. Let stand for 1 hour.

Before serving, toss with 1/2 large head
romaine lettuce, torn into bite-size pieces.
Sprinkle with toasted pitas. *Serves 6 to 8.*

H is for Herbs . . .

The ultimate finishing touch for FRESH HERBED
TOMATO PASTA (see recipe page 56) is tossing it with a
good Parmesan and plenty of garden-fresh herbs.

HERBS

Fresh herbs such as basil or coriander are often the final touch that gives garden-fresh character to any meal. Remember after simmering a dish to add a fresh scattering just before serving.

FRESH HERBED TOMATO PASTA

Cook ½ lb (250 g) linguine or thin flat pasta in boiling salted water until al dente, about 8 min.

Stir **4 chopped seeded tomatoes** with **½ cup grated Parmesan,** **¼ cup chopped fresh basil or ½ tsp dried basil, 1 to 2 tbsp chopped fresh oregano or ½ tsp dried leaf oregano, 1 tbsp olive oil, 2 minced garlic cloves, ½ tsp salt** and **¼ tsp pepper.**

Toss with drained pasta. Sprinkle with **chopped chives.** *Serves 2.*

CLASSIC PESTO

In a food processor, whirl **½ cup pine nuts, 2 minced garlic cloves** and **pinches of salt and pepper.** Whirl, using an on-and-off motion, until a paste forms.

Add **¾ cup grated Parmesan** and **1 cup lightly packed fresh basil leaves.** Continue to whirl until basil is puréed.

While machine is running, gradually add **¾ cup olive oil,** drop by drop at first, then in a thin steady stream.

Use right away or keep refrigerated in a sealed jar for weeks or in the freezer for several months. Spread on pizza or toss with pasta. *Makes 1 cup.*

ACTON'S LEMON-PESTO DRESSING

In a food processor, whirl **1 cup lightly packed fresh basil leaves, 1 tbsp freshly squeezed lemon juice, ½ cup toasted pine nuts, 2 minced garlic cloves** and **½ tsp salt.**

Whirl, using an on-and-off motion, until fairly smooth, scraping down sides of bowl often.

While machine is running, gradually add **½ cup olive oil,** drop by drop at first, then in a thin steady stream.

Taste and whirl in more lemon juice, 1 tbsp at a time, if needed.

Use in potato salad or on greens. *Makes 1 cup.*

JALAPEÑO TOMATO PESTO

In a food processor, whirl until coarsely chopped **½ cup toasted whole almonds** and **4 garlic cloves.**

Add **4 seeded large tomatoes,** cut into chunks, **2 seeded jalapeños, 2 cups packed fresh basil leaves, 1 cup packed parsley leaves, 2 tbsp olive oil** and **1½ tsp salt.** Whirl until very finely chopped.

Add **½ cup grated Parmesan (optional)** and whirl.

Serve as a dip or toss with hot pasta. *Makes 3½ cups.*

Fresh Herbed Scrambled Eggs

FRESH HERBED SCRAMBLED EGGS

Finely chop **3 tbsp** each fresh basil and chives.
  Whisk **12 eggs** with ⅓ **cup milk** and
  ½ **tsp** each salt and pepper.
Melt **3 tbsp** unsalted butter in a large
  frying pan. Add eggs. Sprinkle with
  half the herbs. Cook over medium-heat,
  stirring often, until set.
Sprinkle with remaining herbs. *Serves 4 to 6.*

PARSLEY GARLIC SAUCE

In a 2-cup measuring cup, microwave
  ¼ **cup** butter, **I minced garlic clove**,
  ¼ **tsp** pepper and pinch of salt, uncovered,
  on high, 1 min.
Stir in ¼ **cup** finely chopped fresh parsley
  or coriander.
Serve warm over new potatoes or spinach.
  Makes ⅓ cup.

CORIANDER CUCUMBER-YOGURT SOUP

In a food processor, whirl **2 seeded jalapeños**
  and **I minced garlic clove**.
Add **I coarsely sliced unpeeled English**
  cucumber, **2 coarsely sliced green onions**,
  4 cups loosely packed fresh coriander
  or parsley leaves, **I tbsp olive oil** and
  ¼ **tsp** salt. Whirl until finely chopped
  but not puréed.
Whirl in ½ **cup cold water** or **4 ice cubes**.
  Turn into a bowl. Stir in **2 cups yogurt**.
Serve very cold. *Serves 4.*

FRESH DILL & EGG DIP

Grate or finely chop **2 hard-boiled eggs**.
Stir with ½ **cup light mayonnaise**,
  I tbsp chopped fresh dill or ½ **tsp dried**
  dillweed, **I finely chopped green onion**
  and pinch of cayenne.
Serve with cucumber rounds, Belgium
  endive spears or celery sticks for scooping.
  Makes 1 cup.

HERBS
◆ continued ◆

BASIL-MOZZARELLA BISCUITS

Preheat oven to 450°F (220°C). Stir
2 cups all-purpose flour with
1 tbsp baking powder and ½ tsp salt.
Stir in ⅓ cup chopped fresh basil
or 2 tsp dried basil and
1½ cups grated mozzarella.
Whisk 3 tbsp olive oil with 1 cup milk.
Stir into flour to form a soft dough.
Place dough on a floured surface. With
floured hands, fold dough in half,
flatten slightly and fold in half again.
Pat out to ½-in. (1-cm) thickness.
Cut out biscuits with a 2-in. (5-cm) cutter.
Lay on greased baking sheet. Bake until
golden, from 10 to 12 min.
Makes 16 biscuits.

HERBACEOUS TOMATOES

Stir ⅔ cup fresh bread crumbs with
2 tbsp melted butter, ⅓ cup snipped chives
or thinly sliced green onions and
1 tsp finely chopped fresh rosemary
or ½ tsp dried rosemary, well crushed.
Preheat oven to 450°F (230°C).
Place 4 halved large tomatoes, cored and
seeded, cut-side up, on foil-lined pan.
Lightly sprinkle with salt and pepper.
Spread herb topping over top.
Bake on lowest rack in preheated oven
until topping is golden, from 7 to 10 min.
Serve right away. *Serves 4.*

GREEN SALSA

In a food processor, whirl until finely
chopped 3 sliced green onions with
1 coarsely chopped garlic clove and
½ cup fresh coriander or parsley leaves.
Add 4.5-oz (127-mL) can drained green chilies,
seeded and halved, with 1 tbsp each olive oil
and freshly squeezed lime juice. Whirl,
using an on-and-off motion, until
mixture is chunky. Taste and add
pinches of salt and pepper.
Spoon on tacos or burritos. *Makes ½ cup.*

CREAMY HONEY-MUSTARD SPREAD

Stir ½ cup Dijon with ¼ cup sour cream,
2 tbsp liquid honey, 2 tbsp finely chopped
parsley or snipped chives and
1 tsp crumbled dried rosemary.
Taste and add pepper (optional).
Use right away or cover and refrigerate for
up to a week. Use as a sandwich spread.
Makes ¾ cup.

ZESTY BASIL VINAIGRETTE

Whisk ⅓ cup red wine vinegar with
2 tbsp Dijon, 2 minced garlic cloves and
¼ tsp each salt and pepper.
Whisking constantly, slowly add ¾ to 1 cup
olive oil in a thin steady stream.
Stir in ½ cup coarsely chopped fresh basil.
Toss with mixed green or spinach salad.
Makes 1¼ cups.

PESTO PIZZA APPETIZER

Preheat oven to 425°F (220°C). Pat
1 lb (500 g) pizza dough over a greased
14-in. (35-cm) pizza pan, forming a rim
around edge.
Stir ½ cup pesto (see recipe page 56) with
1 minced large garlic clove and spread
evenly over crust.
Sprinkle with finely chopped sun-dried
tomatoes, red pepper and pimentos.
Sprinkle with 1½ to 2 cups grated Asiago,
Fontina or mozzarella cheese.
Bake immediately on bottom rack of oven
until golden, from 15 to 20 min.
Makes 16 small wedges.

BASIL CHÈVRE SWIRLS

Spread 4 small flour tortillas with
½ cup plain or herbed creamy chèvre
or cream cheese.
Sprinkle with ¼ cup chopped fresh basil
or dill and ¼ tsp pepper.
Snugly roll up and wrap each roll in waxed
paper. Refrigerate until cold.
Unwrap and diagonally slice each into
4 pieces for appetizers. *Makes 16 pieces.*

Basil Chèvre Swirls

L is for Lemons . . .

Lentils, a fast-cooking legume, quickly
meld into a savory sauce in SPINACH,
LENTIL & PASTA TOSS (see recipe page 64).

L

LEMONS

The lemon's appeal lies in its simplicity — its fresh clean tart taste bursts with flavor. Sometimes all it takes is a quick spritz of freshly squeezed juice or a sprinkling of colorful peel to turn an ordinary recipe into something really special.

FRESH LEMONY MAYONNAISE

Whisk 2 tbsp freshly squeezed lemon juice with ¼ cup light mayonnaise, 1 minced small garlic clove and ¼ tsp each salt and freshly ground black pepper.

Drizzle over asparagus, cold poached salmon or sliced tomatoes. Excellent in potato salad, coleslaw or as a dip for fresh vegetables. *Makes ⅓ cup.*

CALIFORNIA CAESAR DRESSING

Whisk 4 tsp freshly squeezed lemon juice with ¼ cup creamy Caesar dressing and a dash of hot pepper sauce.

Drizzle over sliced tomatoes, mixed greens or burgers. Use in tuna salad. *Makes ⅓ cup.*

LEMON-DILL POTATOES

Cook 6 quartered peeled potatoes in boiling salted water until tender, from 15 to 25 min.

Stir 2 tbsp room-temperature butter with finely grated peel of 1 small lemon, 1 tsp freshly squeezed lemon juice and pinches of salt and pepper.

Toss with hot potatoes and 2 to 4 tbsp finely chopped fresh dill. *Serves 4 to 6.*

MEDITERRANEAN VINAIGRETTE

Stir 3 tbsp freshly squeezed lemon juice with ¼ cup olive oil, 1 minced garlic clove and ¼ tsp each cumin and salt.

Stir in pinches of paprika and cayenne.

Fabulous tossed with tomatoes, cucumbers, spinach or grilled vegetables. Also good for pasta or potato salads. *Makes ⅓ cup.*

LEMON TAHINI DRESSING

Stir ¼ cup tahini with 2 tbsp each freshly squeezed lemon juice and water, 2 tbsp finely chopped fresh parsley or coriander, 1 minced garlic clove, ½ tsp salt and ¼ tsp cayenne.

Dab over tomatoes or use as a dip for fresh vegetables. Also great in chicken or egg salads. *Makes ⅓ cup.*

LEMON BUTTER

Stir 1 tsp finely grated lemon peel, 2 tsp freshly squeezed lemon juice and a generous grinding of black pepper into ¼ cup room-temperature butter.

Serve as a zesty topping over vegetables. *Makes ¼ cup.*

Mediterranean Vinaigrette

HERBED LEMON MAYONNAISE

Stir ¼ cup mayonnaise with finely grated
peel of 1 lemon and generous pinches
of dried basil, oregano or tarragon.

Great as a sandwich spread instead of butter.
Makes ¼ cup.

SOUR CREAM & TARRAGON DRESSING

Whisk ½ cup sour cream with 1 tsp each
finely grated lemon peel and freshly
squeezed lemon juice, 1 tsp dried tarragon
and pinches of salt and white pepper.

Whisk in 1 to 2 tbsp milk, 1 tbsp at a time,
until desired consistency is achieved.

Toss with potato or pasta salad. Or use as a
drizzle for tomatoes, cold asparagus,
salmon or grilled chicken. *Makes ½ cup.*

ZESTY LEMON CURD

Whisk 4 egg yolks with 2 whole eggs.
Add ⅔ cup granulated sugar and
⅔ cup freshly squeezed lemon juice,
from about 3 lemons, and ½ cup butter,
cut into small pieces.

Place over low heat, stirring constantly, until
sugar is dissolved. Continue to stir often
for 5 min., then constantly until thick
enough to coat a metal spoon, about
6 more min.

Pour into a bowl and press a piece of clear
wrap onto surface. Refrigerate.

Wonderful as a topping on fresh fruit or
scones or as a cake, pie or tart filling.
Makes 2 cups.

LENTILS

Lentils are quick-cooking legumes whose nutritional protein profile make them particularly attractive to vegetarians. Sold dried or canned, they quickly cook to form a healthy base for purées, soups and salads.

SPINACH, LENTIL & PASTA TOSS

Sauté 1 coarsely chopped red onion and 4 minced large garlic cloves in 2 tbsp olive oil until softened, about 5 min.

Stir in ¾ cup rinsed brown lentils, 1½ cups chicken or vegetable broth, 1 tsp dried basil, ½ tsp each dried oregano and salt and ¼ tsp cayenne. Bring to a boil. Partially cover and simmer for 15 min.

Add 19-oz can undrained tomatoes. Break up tomatoes. Boil gently, uncovered, to thicken, 10 min.

Cook 1 lb (450 g) macaroni or penne in boiling salted water until al dente, about 10 min. Drain.

Stir 10-oz (284-mL) bag torn spinach into sauce. When wilted, toss with hot pasta and ½ cup freshly grated Asiago or Fontina. *Serves 6 to 8.*

VEGGIE & LENTIL SALAD

Combine ½ (19-oz) can rinsed well-drained lentils or 1 cup cooked lentils with 1 cup chopped vegetables, such as celery, carrots and peppers.

Stir ¼ tsp each curry powder and salt into ¼ cup sour cream, then stir into salad. *Serves 1 to 2.*

INTRIGUING LENTIL SOUP

In a large saucepan, place 1 cup rinsed green or brown lentils, 1 coarsely chopped large onion, 3 minced garlic cloves, 2 tsp curry powder, ⅛ tsp hot red pepper flakes, 2 cups water, 2 (10-oz) cans undiluted chicken broth or 2½ cups vegetable broth. Cover and bring to a boil over high heat.

Reduce heat and boil gently until lentils are very soft, from 20 to 25 min.

Swirl a large dollop of yogurt into each bowl of soup. *Serves 4 to 6.*

SPEEDY LENTIL CHILI

Sauté 1 chopped small onion and 2 minced garlic cloves in 1½ tsp olive oil or butter until soft, about 5 min.

Stir 1 tbsp all-purpose flour with 1 tbsp chili powder, 1½ tsp cumin and ¼ tsp each salt and cayenne. Sprinkle over onions and stir for 2 min.

Stir in 19-oz can undrained Mexican-style stewed tomatoes, 19-oz can rinsed drained lentils and 2 tbsp canned diced green chilies or 1 finely chopped seeded jalapeño. Bring to a boil.

Partially cover and simmer, stirring often to blend flavors, about 15 min. Serve with warm tortillas or hot rice. *Serves 4.*

LENTIL PURÉE SOUP

Purée 19-oz can lentils, including juice,
  with 1 minced large garlic clove and
  ¼ tsp cayenne.
Heat with 1 cup chicken or vegetable
  bouillon or stock until hot. *Serves 2 to 3.*

MEDITERRANEAN LENTIL SALAD

Combine 1 cup rinsed green or brown
  lentils and 6 cups water. Bring to a boil.
  Simmer until lentils are tender, from
  20 to 25 min. Drain well.
Sauté 1 finely chopped onion, 2 minced
  garlic cloves, 1 tsp cumin and ½ tsp salt
  in 1 tbsp olive oil until onion has softened,
  about 5 min.
Stir into drained lentils with 1½ tsp balsamic
  or red wine vinegar. When cooled,
  stir in 1 chopped sweet pepper and
  ½ cup chopped fresh coriander.
  Serves 3 to 4.

CREOLE LENTIL SOUP

Sauté 1 chopped large onion and
  2 chopped celery stalks in
  2 tbsp butter for 5 min.
Stirring constantly, sprinkle vegetables
  with ¼ cup all-purpose flour, then slowly
  whisk in 4 cups chicken or vegetable broth.
  Stir until mixture starts to thicken.
Add 1 cup red lentils, ¼ tsp each dried leaf
  thyme, pepper and hot red pepper sauce
  and 1 bay leaf. Bring to a boil.
Skim off foam. Cover and simmer until
  lentils are tender, from 20 to 25 min.
  Stir occasionally.
Stir in 1 to 2 chopped seeded tomatoes
  and 1 to 2 chopped red peppers.
  Remove bay leaf. Taste and add salt and
  more hot sauce if needed. *Serves 7 to 8.*

Spinach, Lentil & Pasta Toss

M is for Mushrooms . . .

Sumptuous sautéed portobello mushrooms are
spritzed with a sesame and balsamic vinegar in
WARM PORTOBELLO & ONION SALAD (see recipe
page 68). Serve on a bed of baby spinach.

MUSHROOMS

The mushroom's mysterious woodsy nature comes from its origin as a fungus rather than a true vegetable. Meaty portobellos, sturdy shiitakes and mild buttons are widely available and can be used in pastas, stir-fries and salads.

WARM PORTOBELLO & ONION SALAD

Whisk 1 tbsp each olive oil and sesame oil with 3 tbsp balsamic vinegar, 1 tsp Dijon and ½ tsp each salt and pepper. Stir in ¼ cup shredded fresh basil.

Heat 2 tbsp olive oil in a large frying pan. When very hot, add 5 to 8 portobello mushrooms, cut into ¼-in. (0.5-cm) thick slices, and 1 sliced small red onion. Stir-fry from 3 to 5 min.

Stir in dressing. Immediately toss with 10-oz (284-g) bag baby spinach leaves and 6 sliced green onions. *Serves 4.*

MUSHROOM PARSLEY PILAF

Sauté 1 chopped onion in 1 tbsp vegetable oil until softened, about 5 min.

Stir in 1 cup rice. Cook, stirring often, about 1 min.

Add 2 cups chicken or vegetable broth, 4 cups sliced button or mixed mushrooms and ½ tsp dried leaf thyme.

Bring to a boil. Cover and simmer, stirring occasionally, 25 min.

Stir in ¼ cup chopped fresh parsley. *Serves 4 to 5.*

CREAMY SPINACH-MUSHROOM SALAD

Toss 2 (10-oz/284-g) bags spinach with 2 cups thinly sliced mushrooms and 1 cup alfalfa or bean sprouts (optional).

Combine ½ cup light or regular sour cream with 2 tbsp milk, 1 tsp red wine vinegar, ½ tsp dried dillweed and pinches of salt and pepper to taste. Toss dressing with salad and serve. *Serves 6 to 8.*

WARM MUSHROOM SPINACH SALAD

Combine 10-oz (284-g) bag baby spinach with 1 grated carrot and ¼ sliced red onion.

Stir-fry 2 sliced portobello mushrooms or ½ lb (125 g) sliced mushrooms in 1 tbsp olive oil for 3 min.

Whisk 1 tbsp olive oil with 3 tbsp balsamic vinegar or lemon juice and generous pinches of salt and pepper.

Stir into hot mushrooms and toss with salad. *Serves 3 to 4.*

TINA'S PORTOBELLO "STEAKS"

Whisk 1 tbsp each soy sauce, Worcestershire sauce and liquid honey.

Brush both sides of 4 large portobello mushroom caps with soy mixture.

Barbecue until richly brown with visible grill marks, about 3 min. per side.

Serve in buns with Fontina or other sliced cheese or with barbecued burgers or steaks. *Serves 4.*

MUSHROOM
RISOTTO

MEATY MUSHROOM STIR-FRY

Sauté 2 minced garlic cloves, 1 tsp minced
fresh ginger or 2 tsp bottled minced ginger
and ½ tsp hot red pepper flakes in
1 tbsp vegetable oil. Stir often over
low heat, 5 min.

Add ¾ lb (375 g) thinly sliced portobello
mushrooms and 1 thinly sliced cooking
onion. Stir-fry over medium heat, 3 min.

Add 2 sliced sweet peppers,
½ thickly sliced bok choy (optional)
and 4 cups broccoli florets. Stir-fry
over medium-high, until broccoli turns
bright green, about 2 min.

Stir in ⅓ cup teriyaki sauce and
2 cups cubed tofu (optional).
Serve over hot rice. *Serves 4 to 6.*

MUSHROOM RISOTTO

Sauté 1 finely chopped onion and 1 minced
garlic clove in 1 tbsp butter for 3 min.

Stir in 1¼ cups short-grain rice, preferably
Arborio, until coated. While constantly
stirring, add 1 cup finely chopped
mushrooms, ½ cup dry white wine and
¼ tsp each salt and hot red pepper flakes.
Stir often until wine is absorbed.

Gradually stir in 10-oz can undiluted chicken
broth or 1¼ cups vegetable broth.

Add 2½ cups water, half a cup at a time,
stirring until all liquid is absorbed
before adding more. Stop adding when
rice is tender and sauce creamy, about
25 min. Stir in ¼ cup each grated
Parmesan and chopped parsley.
Add salt to taste. *Serves 3 to 4.*

MUSHROOMS
◆ *continued* ◆

ITALIAN MUSHROOMS & PIMENTOS

Boil 1 lb (500 g) mushrooms for 30 seconds. Immediately drain, pat dry and slice.

Combine with 4 thinly sliced green onions and ¼ cup chopped pimentos.

Whisk ⅓ cup olive oil with 3 tbsp red wine vinegar, 2 minced garlic cloves, 3 tbsp chopped fresh basil or 1 tsp dried basil, 1 tbsp fresh oregano leaves or ½ tsp dried oregano, ½ tsp salt and pinch of pepper.

Pour over mushroom mixture and gently toss. *Serves 4 to 6.*

ROQUEFORT & MUSHROOM SALAD

Whisk ¼ cup olive oil with 2 tbsp balsamic vinegar, 1 minced garlic clove, ¼ tsp each salt and pepper.

Stir in ½ lb (250 g) thickly sliced mushrooms, ¼ cup chopped fresh basil or 1 tsp dried basil and 1 tbsp chopped fresh oregano or ¼ tsp dried oregano.

Tear 1 large head romaine lettuce into bite-size pieces. Toss with mushroom mixture. Add 1 thinly sliced red pepper and ½ to 1 cup crumbled Roquefort or other blue cheese. *Serves 8.*

MARINATED GARLIC MUSHROOMS

Whisk ¼ cup olive oil with 1 tbsp red wine vinegar, 1 minced garlic clove, ½ tsp dried oregano and pinches of salt and pepper.

Stir in ½ lb (250 g) small whole mushrooms. Refrigerate for a day to marinate. *Makes 2 cups.*

CREAMY MUSHROOM PASTA

Heat 1 tbsp each butter and olive oil. Add 2 finely chopped shallots and sauté for 1 min.

Add 1 lb (500 g) sliced mushrooms and 2 tbsp Madeira, dry sherry or port. Sauté, uncovered, until most of liquid has evaporated, about 10 min.

Add 1 cup whipping cream and 3 cups chopped spinach. Boil mixture gently until thickened slightly, about 5 min.

Add pinches of salt and pepper. Toss with 12 oz (375 g) cooked broad egg noodles and lots of grated Parmesan. *Serves 6.*

OYSTER MUSHROOMS & SNOW PEAS

Stir 1 tbsp each soy sauce and rice wine vinegar with 1 tsp dark sesame oil and ¼ tsp each salt and granulated sugar.

Heat 1 tbsp vegetable oil over high heat. Add 4 cups thickly sliced oyster mushrooms. Stir-fry for 2 min.

Add 1 cup sliced snow peas and soy mixture. Stir-fry until peas are hot, about 1 min.

Serve over hot rice. *Serves 4.*

GINGER-MUSHROOM SAUTÉ

Heat 1 tbsp each butter and vegetable oil. Add 1 lb (500 g) sliced mushrooms, 1 tbsp soy sauce, 2 thinly sliced green onions and 2 tsp minced fresh ginger.

Sauté until mushrooms are tender, about 5 min. Season with pinches of salt and pepper. *Serves 4.*

Southwestern Mushroom Tacos

Sauté **3 to 4** unpeeled new potatoes, cut into ½-in. (1-cm) chunks, in **1 tbsp** olive oil, until golden, about **20 min.** Remove from pan.

Add another **1 tbsp** olive oil and sauté **1** thinly sliced onion, **1** thinly sliced green or red pepper and **4 minced** garlic cloves for **5 min.**

Add **1 lb (500 g)** quartered large mushrooms, **1½ tsp** chili powder, **1 tsp** each cumin and salt and **¼ tsp** pepper. Continue cooking until most moisture has evaporated, about **5 min.**

Stir in potatoes and heat through. Stir in **¼ cup** chopped fresh coriander.

Warm **8 small tortillas.** Spoon in potato-mushroom mixture. Top with sour cream and roll up. *Serves 4.*

Laughing Moon's Breakfast

Sauté **1** finely chopped onion and **1** minced garlic clove in **1 tbsp** vegetable oil for **3 min.** Add **1** finely chopped green pepper and **1 cup** sliced mushrooms. Stir frequently for **3 min.**

Add **¾ cup** salsa and bring to a boil. Then reduce heat so mixture gently bubbles. Stir frequently, especially as it thickens, about **5 min.** Remove from heat.

Meanwhile, fry **4 eggs** until softly set.

Place **2 toasted bagels,** sliced in half, on a baking sheet. Top each half with an egg and hot salsa mixture.

Sprinkle with **1 cup** grated cheddar. Broil until cheese melts, about **2 min.** *Serves 4.*

Southwestern Mushroom Tacos

O is for Olives . .

This handsome aromatic SPANISH TOSS
(see recipe page 75), made with ingredients you
may already have on hand, is ready in 10 minutes.

A B C D E F G H I J K L M N O P Q R S T U V W X Y Z

OLIVE OIL

Olive oils, often with virgin designation, can be almost as intriguing as a fine wine. Here's a list of ways to enjoy their complexities. Save your best for dishes where the olive taste will shine and use a less expensive variety for frying.

CLASSIC VINAIGRETTE

Whisk ½ cup olive oil with 3 to 4 tbsp freshly squeezed lemon juice or white or balsamic vinegar, 1 tsp Dijon and ¼ tsp each salt and pepper.

Toss with greens, pasta or potato salad. *Makes 1 cup.*

HERBED CHEESE VINAIGRETTE

Whisk ½ cup olive oil with 3 to 4 tbsp freshly squeezed lemon juice or white or balsamic vinegar, 1 minced large garlic clove, generous pinches of chopped fresh or dried herbs, such as basil, oregano or parsley, and dashes of hot pepper sauce.

Add 2 to 3 tbsp crumbled feta or Roquefort or whisk in ¼ cup freshly grated Parmesan or Romano. *Makes 1 cup.*

HONEY-DIJON TOMATOES

Whisk 2 tbsp Dijon with 2 tbsp olive oil, 2 tsp liquid honey and 2 tsp white wine or cider vinegar. Drizzle over 4 sliced tomatoes. *Serves 4.*

GARLICKY SPREAD

Stir ½ cup olive oil with ½ cup room-temperature butter and 2 to 4 minced large garlic cloves.

The oil keeps spread soft enough to spread straight from the refrigerator onto bread or vegetables. Great for garlic bread. Keep refrigerated up to a week or freeze.

Add 2 tbsp chopped parsley (optional). *Makes 1 cup.*

HERBED CHEESE APPETIZER

Stir 3 tbsp olive oil with 2 tbsp chopped fresh basil or parsley, 1 minced garlic clove and pinches of pepper and cayenne.

Pour over 2 cups cubed mozzarella or feta.

Leave at room temperature up to 3 hours or refrigerate up to 1 week.

Serve with crackers or bread. *Makes 2 cups.*

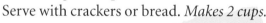

Honey-Dijon Tomatoes

OLIVES

*From the briny wine-cured tiny black to large cracked green globes,
olives have finally leaped from the appetizer tray to earthy pasta sauces, flavor-filled
spreads, pizzas and Mediterranean-style salads.*

SPANISH TOSS

Whisk ½ cup olive oil with 2 tbsp red
   wine vinegar, 2 minced large garlic cloves
   and 1 tsp dried leaf thyme.
Slice 1 cup stuffed green olives and chop
   4 seeded tomatoes. Stir into oil mixture.
Toss with about 1 lb (450 g) cooked drained
   pasta or cheese tortellini. *Serves 6 to 8.*

TAPENADE

In a food processor, whirl until finely chopped
   1 cup pitted black olives with
   1 tbsp drained capers,
   2 tbsp freshly squeezed lemon juice,
   1 tbsp olive oil, 2 tbsp brandy, 1 tsp Dijon,
   ¼ tsp dried leaf thyme and ¼ tsp pepper.
Thinly spread over grilled bread slices or
   substitute for tomato sauce when making
   pizza or toss with hot pasta. Covered and
   refrigerated, tapenade will keep well for up
   to a week. *Makes ¾ cup.*

LIGHT MEDITERRANEAN OLIVE SALAD

In a food processor, whirl ½ cup crumbled
   feta cheese with 2 tbsp milk, 1 tbsp freshly
   squeezed lemon juice, 1 tbsp olive oil and
   ½ tsp each dried oregano and dried basil.
   Thin with milk, adding 1 tbsp at a time
   until pourable.
Toss with sliced or diced tomatoes, small
   black olives and shredded romaine.
   Makes ½ cup.

CREOLE OLIVE & TOMATO SALAD

Stir 12 finely chopped stuffed green olives
   with 4 coarsely chopped large tomatoes.
Whisk ¼ cup olive oil with 1 tbsp red or
   white wine vinegar, ¼ tsp each dried leaf
   thyme, basil and salt and pinches of
   cayenne. Toss with tomatoes. *Serves 4.*

OLIVE PIZZA

Preheat oven to 400°F (200°C). Place
   1 store-bought pizza crust on a baking
   sheet. Spoon ¾ cup salsa evenly over crust.
Scatter with ½ cup sliced pitted black olives.
Sprinkle with 1 cup each grated mozzarella
   and Asiago. Bake on bottom rack of oven
   until cheese is golden, about 18 min.
   Makes 6 wedges.

JALAPEÑO-OLIVE SALSA

Stir 3 coarsely chopped seeded tomatoes
   with ¼ cup slivered black olives,
   ¼ cup thinly sliced green onions,
   1 minced garlic clove and
   1 tbsp minced seeded jalapeño.
Whisk 3 tbsp olive oil with 1 tbsp red
   wine vinegar, ½ tsp granulated sugar
   and pinches of salt and pepper.
Stir with tomatoes. Great spooned into
   bean burritos or with scrambled eggs.
   Makes 1½ cups.

P is for Peppers . . . .

Serve a crowd in less than 30 minutes with
Orzo & Spinach Gremolada Salad (see recipe page 78).
A fresh garlic and parsley mixture adds lots of flavor.

PASTA

Pasta tossed with assorted veggies is the weekday dinner of choice for many busy people.
Here are new ways to dress and embellish it that includes
delicate orzo stuffed into tomatoes and spinach rolled in lasagna noodles.

ORZO & SPINACH GREMOLADA SALAD

Cook 2 cups orzo pasta in boiling salted
water until al dente, about 8 min.

Whisk 3 tbsp olive oil with 3 tbsp freshly
squeezed lemon juice, 2 minced garlic
cloves and $\frac{1}{4}$ tsp each salt and pepper.

Stir in drained orzo. Add 1 bunch spinach or
$\frac{1}{2}$ (10-oz/284-g) bag spinach, torn into
pieces, and $\frac{1}{4}$ cup sliced pitted black olives.

Stir $\frac{1}{4}$ cup finely chopped parsley with
$\frac{1}{2}$ tsp each finely grated orange and
lemon peel.

Sprinkle over mixture and serve. *Serves 8.*

LIGHT & CREAMY TOMATO LINGUINE

Cook $\frac{1}{4}$ lb (125 g) linguine in boiling salted
water until al dente, about 8 min.

Sauté $\frac{1}{2}$ cup finely diced red onion and
4 minced large garlic cloves in
1 tsp olive oil, for 2 min.

Add 2 diced large tomatoes, $\frac{1}{2}$ cup tomato
juice, 4 black olives and 1 tsp capers.

Gently boil, uncovered and stirring often,
until half of liquid is reduced, about 5 min.

Stir in 4 oz (125 g) ricotta cheese or grated
Parmesan and toss with hot drained pasta.
Serves 2 to 3.

VENETIAN STUFFED TOMATOES

Cook $1\frac{1}{2}$ cups orzo pasta in boiling salted
water until al dente, about 8 min.

Slice $\frac{1}{2}$-in. (1-cm) thick piece off tops
of 6 large tomatoes. Scoop out pulp.
Discard seeds and juice. Chop and
place in a bowl. Turn shells upside
down on paper towels to drain.

Add drained pasta to tomato pulp with
$\frac{1}{2}$ cup pesto (see recipe page 56)
$\frac{1}{4}$ cup olive oil and $\frac{1}{4}$ tsp pepper.
Spoon into tomato halves.

Sprinkle with finely chopped fresh basil.
Serves 6.

RAVIOLI WITH HERBED SAUCE

Cook $\frac{1}{2}$ lb (250 g) ravioli in boiling salted
water until al dente, from 4 to 6 min.

Sauté 2 minced garlic cloves in
2 tbsp olive oil, 3 min.

Add 2 chopped seeded tomatoes. Sprinkle
with 2 tbsp finely chopped fresh basil or
1 tsp dried basil and $\frac{1}{2}$ tsp dried oregano.

Remove from heat. Toss with drained pasta.

Sprinkle with grated Parmesan and
pinches of salt and pepper. *Serves 2.*

Spinach Lasagna Rolls

CAPELLINI WITH HOT CHILIES

Cook 1 lb (450 g) capellini in boiling salted
water until al dente, about 5 min.

Heat ⅓ cup olive oil with ½ tsp hot red
pepper flakes and 6 minced garlic cloves.

Simmer over medium-low heat, stirring
occasionally, until pasta is ready.

Toss with drained pasta. Add 1 cup chopped
parsley and 1 cup grated Parmesan.
Serves 4.

PESTO CHÈVRE FETTUCCINE

Cook 1 lb (450 g) fettuccine in boiling salted
water until al dente, about 8 min.

Heat 2 cups spaghetti sauce with
1 finely chopped green pepper,
1 tsp dried basil and ¼ tsp cayenne.

Crumble ½ to 1 cup creamy chèvre into
sauce and stir until melted.

Toss with drained pasta. *Serves 4.*

SPINACH LASAGNA ROLLS

Cook 8 lasagna noodles in boiling salted
water for 8 min.

Steam or microwave 2 bunches fresh spinach
or 10-oz (284-g) bag spinach until wilted
or hot, about 3 min. Drain and squeeze.

In a food processor, whirl spinach with
½ lb (250 g) ricotta cheese,
¼ cup grated Parmesan, ¼ tsp pepper
and pinches of nutmeg and salt.

Preheat oven to 350°F (180°C).

Spread ¼ cup cheese mixture over each
drained lasagna noodle. Roll up jelly-roll
fashion, then set seam-side down in
greased 9x9-in. (2.5-L) baking dish. Cover
tightly and bake until hot, about 25 min.

Top with 1 cup heated spaghetti sauce.
Serves 3 to 4.

PASTA
• *continued* •

GARLIC-CHILI PASTA

Cook 1 lb (500 g) cheese tortellini or ravioli in boiling salted water until al dente, from 4 to 6 min.

Sauté ¼ to ½ tsp hot red pepper flakes and 3 minced garlic cloves in ¼ cup olive oil.

Stir often so oil will take on garlic and chili flavors, about 5 min.

Toss with pasta until evenly coated. Sprinkle with fresh parsley or coriander (optional). *Serves 4.*

MODERN MAC & CHEESE

Cook 1 lb (450 g) elbow macaroni in boiling salted water until al dente, about 10 min.

Combine ½ cup partly skimmed ricotta cheese with ¼ cup 2% milk, ½ tsp pepper, ¼ tsp salt and pinch of cayenne.

Stir in 1 cup each grated Jarlsberg and mozzarella, ½ cup grated Parmesan and 3 tbsp finely chopped parsley.

Toss with drained pasta. *Serves 6 to 8.*

PASTA WITH TOMATOES & HOT PEPPERS

Cook ¾ lb (375 g) fettuccine in boiling salted water until al dente, about 8 min.

Combine 28-oz can drained plum tomatoes with 3 finely chopped seeded jalapeños or 4.5-oz (127-mL) can drained chopped green chilies, 2 tbsp olive oil, 2 minced garlic cloves and generous pinches of thyme, marjoram and salt. Bring to a boil. Cover and simmer, stirring often, 10 min.

Toss with drained pasta. Sprinkle with grated Romano or Parmesan. *Serves 3 to 4.*

TOMATO TORTELLINI FOR TWO

Cook ½ lb (250 g) tortellini in boiling salted water until al dente, from 4 to 6 min.

Stir 4 coarsely chopped tomatoes with 2 sliced green onions, 1 to 2 minced garlic cloves, 1 tsp granulated sugar, ½ tsp pepper and ¼ tsp cayenne (optional).

Drain pasta. Return to pan and crumble in ½ cup Roquefort or Stilton cheese.

Stir over low heat until the cheese begins to melt. Add tomato mixture. Stir gently until hot. *Serves 2.*

HERBED PASTA SALAD

Cook 1 lb (450 g) penne in boiling salted water until al dente, about 10 min.

Whisk ⅓ cup vegetable oil with finely grated peel and juice of 1 orange, 1 minced garlic clove, ½ tsp salt, 1 tbsp chopped fresh sage leaves or ¼ tsp dried sage and pinches of pepper.

Add 1 julienned yellow pepper, 1 sliced red onion and 2 cups small cherry tomatoes.

Toss with drained pasta. Refrigerate until cold. *Serves 6 to 8.*

RIGATONI WITH GORGONZOLA

Cook ½ lb (250 g) rigatoni in boiling salted water until al dente, about 10 min.

Cube 4 oz (125 g) room-temperature Gorgonzola or Cambozola. Toss with drained pasta and 2 tbsp butter.

Sprinkle with grated Parmesan and ½ cup toasted hazelnuts or walnuts. Add salt and pepper to taste. *Serves 2 to 4.*

MILD & TERRIFIC TORTELLINI

Sauté 1 coarsely chopped onion and
1 large garlic clove, cut in half, in
2 tbsp olive oil, about 5 min.
Add 4 chopped large tomatoes,
4 large fresh basil leaves and
$\frac{1}{2}$ tsp salt. Bring to a boil. Reduce heat
and simmer, uncovered, stirring often
until thickened, about 25 min.
Purée tomato sauce in a food processor.
Cook 1 lb (500 g) tortellini or ravioli in
boiling salted water until al dente, from
4 to 6 min. Toss with tomato sauce.
Sprinkle with grated Parmesan. *Serves 4.*

SUMMER PASTA TOSS

Cook 1 lb (450 g) penne in boiling
salted water until al dente, about 10 min.
Sauté 1 thinly sliced zucchini,
1 julienned sweet pepper and
pinches of salt and pepper in
$\frac{1}{4}$ cup olive oil until tender-crisp,
about 3 min.
Toss with drained pasta. Add 2 chopped
tomatoes, 2 sliced green onions,
$\frac{1}{4}$ cup chopped fresh basil and
$\frac{1}{4}$ tsp each salt and pepper.
Sprinkle with grated Parmesan.
Serves 4.

SUMMER PASTA TOSS

ABCDEFGHIJKLMNOPQRSTUVWXYZ

PEPPERS

*There are often more varieties of peppers sold in supermarkets today than potatoes.
Whether you roast, toss or sauté them, all are stars in supplying healthy beta-carotene.*

PESTO PEPPER PENNE

Sauté **1 sliced red pepper** and **1 sliced onion** in **1 tsp olive oil**.

When softened, toss with **½ cup pesto** (see recipe page 56) and **4 cups hot cooked penne**.

Season with **salt, pepper and hot red pepper flakes**. Sprinkle with **grated Parmesan**.
Serves 4.

TRI-PEPPER FETTUCCINE

Cook **1 lb (450 g) fettuccine** in boiling salted water until al dente, about 8 min.

Sauté **1 each julienned green, red and yellow peppers**, **1 minced large garlic clove**, **1½ tsp Italian seasoning** and pinches of salt and pepper in **3 tbsp olive oil** until tender, about 8 min.

Stir in **½ cup pitted black olives**.

Toss with drained pasta and **1 cup grated Parmesan**. Sprinkle with **chopped parsley**.
Serves 4 to 6.

FRESH HOT PEPPER SAUCE

In a food processor, whirl **3 sliced seeded jalapeños or hot banana peppers** with **1 coarsely chopped onion** and **1 large garlic clove**.

Add **⅓ cup freshly squeezed lime or lemon juice**. Whirl until blended.

Good drizzled over nachos. *Makes 1 cup.*

GRILLED PEPPER RELISH

Preheat barbecue and oil grill. Cut **3 sweet peppers, a mix of colors**, in half and seed.

Stir **3 tbsp freshly squeezed lemon juice** with **3 tbsp olive oil**, **1 minced garlic clove** and **¼ tsp each salt and pepper**. Lightly brush over peppers, saving remaining mixture.

Grill peppers until singed on edges but still firm, from 15 to 20 min. Then coarsely chop. Stir with remaining mixture. Add **2 finely chopped jalapeños** and **¼ cup chopped fresh coriander**.

Great with couscous, chicken or fish steaks.
Makes 2 cups.

QUICK & EASY PIZZA

Preheat oven to 425°F (220°C). Pat **1 lb (500 g) pizza dough** over a greased 14-in. (35-cm) pizza pan, forming a rim around edge.

Arrange **1 each julienned small red, green and yellow peppers** and **6 sliced mushrooms** over top.

Sprinkle with **¼ cup finely chopped fresh basil** or **½ tsp dried basil**, **1½ cups grated mozzarella** and pinch of pepper.

Bake on bottom rack until golden, from 15 to 20 min. *Makes 8 wedges.*

*ROASTED
RED PEPPER
SOUP*

RED PEPPER RAVIOLI

Cook 1 lb (450 g) ravioli in boiling salted
water until al dente, from 4 to 6 min.

Sauté **3 minced garlic cloves** in 1 tbsp olive oil,
about 3 min.

In a food processor, whirl cooked garlic with
**2 roasted red peppers or 7½-oz (250-mL)
jar drained roasted red peppers**. Whirl
until smooth.

Toss drained pasta with 1 tbsp olive oil.

Spread red pepper purée over four dinner
plates. Arrange ravioli over top.

Sprinkle with **sliced green onions or chives.**
Serves 4.

ROASTED RED PEPPER SOUP

Sauté **2 minced garlic cloves** and **2 chopped
onions** in **2 tbsp olive oil** until soft,
about 8 min.

Stir in **4 large roasted red peppers or
2 (7½-oz/250-mL) jars roasted red peppers**,
cut into chunks. Cook until peppers are
very soft. Then purée.

Stir into **3 cups chicken or vegetable broth.**
Heat until hot. *Serves 6 to 8.*

FAST PEPPER STIR-FRY

Stir-fry 1 thinly sliced large garlic clove
with **3 chopped sweet peppers** and
1 sliced zucchini in **2 tbsp olive oil**, 2 min.

Add ¼ cup **Italian or Caesar dressing** and
freshly ground black pepper.

Serve with **grated Parmesan.** *Serves 3 to 4.*

POTATOES

Potatoes top the veggie hit parade (sometimes it's the only vegetable kids willingly eat).
Check out our homey to posh ways to liven up this most satisfying of tubers.

POTATO PARMIGIANA STIR-FRY

In a large pan, stir-fry **1 sliced large garlic clove**
in **2 tbsp vegetable oil**, 2 min., then
discard garlic.

Slice **4 unpeeled medium potatoes** into
½-in. (1-cm) wedges and add to oil.
Stir-fry over medium-high heat until
golden, about 8 to 12 min.

Add **1 julienned red pepper**,
2 thinly sliced zucchini,
1 thinly sliced onion, **½ tsp dried basil** and
pinch of pepper. Stir-fry until vegetables
are tender-crisp, from 5 to 8 min.

Remove from heat and stir in
1 cup grated Parmesan until melted.
Serves 4.

POTATO SCONES

Preheat oven to 425°F (220°C). Stir
1¼ **cups all-purpose flour** with
¼ **cup granulated sugar**,
1 tbsp baking powder and **1 tsp salt**.
Cut in ⅓ **cup cold butter**.

Whisk ⅓ **cup milk** with **1 whole egg** and
1 egg yolk. Stir in ¾ **cup moist mashed**
potatoes. Stir into flour mixture.
Do not overmix.

Turn onto a lightly floured board. Knead
briefly. Pat into ½-in. (1-cm) thick circle.
Cut into 8 wedges. Bake 2 in. (5 cm) apart
on an ungreased baking sheet until golden,
from 12 to 15 min. *Makes 8 scones.*

SESAME POTATOES

Preheat oven to 425°F (220°C). Slice
4 unpeeled potatoes in half. Rub with
1 tbsp sesame oil. Generously sprinkle with
coarsely ground black pepper and **salt**.

Bake on a baking sheet until tender, about
45 min. Turn partway through. *Serves 4.*

TWICE-BAKED ITALIAN POTATOES

Preheat oven to 400°F (200°C). Bake
4 oiled unpeeled potatoes until tender,
from 45 to 55 min. Slice in half.

Scoop pulp into a dish, reserving skin.
Mash in **2 tbsp olive oil**, **1 minced large**
garlic clove, **1 tsp dried basil** and
½ **tsp dried oregano**.

Stir in **2 cups grated mozzarella**. Mound in
potato skins.

Sprinkle with **1 cup grated mozzarella**.
Bake until hot and golden, 15 min.
Serves 4 to 6.

SPICY POTATO WEDGES

Preheat oven to 425°F (220°C). Slice
4 unpeeled potatoes into ½-in. (1-cm)
wedges. Drizzle with **1 tbsp olive** or
vegetable oil. Sprinkle with **salt**, **pepper**
and **cayenne**.

Toss, then spread out on a greased baking
sheet. Bake in oven for 15 min. Turn
potatoes and bake until golden, about
20 more min. *Serves 4.*

CHEESY MASHED POTATOES

Cook **8** quartered peeled medium potatoes in boiling water until very tender, about 25 minutes. Drain and mash.

Stir in **1** tbsp butter, **½** cup sour cream, **1** tsp salt and **¼** tsp pepper.

Mix in **1** cup grated cheddar. Sprinkle with sliced green onions. *Serves 6 to 8.*

MINI ROSEMARY POTATOES

In a frying pan, cook **2** cups peeled small round potatoes in boiling water until almost tender, from **8** to **10** min. Drain.

Add **2** tbsp butter. Crumble in **1** tsp rosemary. Stir continuously over high heat until golden.

Sprinkle with salt and pepper. *Serves 2.*

HERBED POTATOES

Cook **8** quartered unpeeled potatoes in boiling water until tender, about **25** min.

Drain potatoes and place in a large bowl.

Add **¼** cup olive oil, **½** tsp dried basil, **¼** tsp pepper and **4** thinly sliced green onions. Toss and serve. *Serves 8.*

CREAMY CELERIAC MASHED POTATOES

Cook **8** quartered peeled potatoes, **1** cubed peeled small celeriac or **2** parsnips, **4** garlic cloves and **½** tsp salt in boiling water until very tender, about 25 minutes. Drain.

Remove garlic and mash with a fork. Return to potatoes. Then mash mixture with a potato masher.

Beat in **¾** cup buttermilk, **¾** tsp salt and pinch of pepper. *Serves 6 to 8.*

SAGE 'N' GARLIC MASHED POTATOES

Cook **6** quartered peeled potatoes and **4** whole garlic cloves in boiling water until tender, from **20** to **25** minutes. Drain.

Remove garlic and mash with a fork. Return to potatoes. Then mash mixture with a potato masher.

Stir in **1** tbsp butter, **½** tsp salt, **¼** tsp crumbled dried sage, **¼** tsp white pepper and **½** cup buttermilk or sour cream. *Serves 6 to 8.*

Spicy Potato Wedges

POTATOES
◆ continued ◆

SKILLET SCALLOPED POTATOES

Combine **8** thinly sliced peeled potatoes with 1½ cups milk, I minced garlic clove, **3 tbsp** butter and ¼ **tsp each** salt and pepper in a saucepan. Bring to a boil.

Cover, reduce heat and simmer until potatoes are tender, about 15 min. Stir often. If mixture becomes too thick, add a little extra milk.

Preheat broiler. Stir ½ **cup grated Swiss or Gruyère cheese** into potatoes. Turn into greased 8-in. (2-L) baking dish.

Top with I **cup grated Swiss.** Broil until golden, about 5 min. *Serves 6 to 8.*

PIZZA POTATO CAKES

Preheat oven to 450°F (230°C). Pat **2 cups mashed potatoes** into 4 small rounds about ½ in. (1 cm) thick on an oiled baking sheet.

Sprinkle with **grated cheese** and pinches of **Italian seasonings** or **basil** and **oregano.**

Bake until cheese is golden, about 20 min. *Makes 4.*

POTATO & WATERCRESS SALAD

Cook **3 lbs (1.5 kg)** small new potatoes in boiling water until tender, about 20 min.

Whisk ⅓ **cup olive oil** with ¼ **cup cider** or **red wine vinegar,** I **tsp Dijon,** I minced garlic clove and ¼ tsp each salt and pepper.

Toss with hot drained potatoes and I diced red pepper.

Before serving hot or at room temperature, stir in ½ **bunch** coarsely chopped **watercress.** *Serves 6.*

ROMAN POTATO SALAD

Cook **8** unpeeled medium potatoes in boiling water until tender, about 25 min.

Whisk ½ **cup olive oil** with **3 tbsp balsamic** or **red wine vinegar, 3 minced garlic cloves,** I **tsp each** salt and **dried basil** and ½ **tsp each hot red pepper flakes** and **dried oregano.**

Stir in I **cup thinly sliced celery** and **2** coarsely chopped **sweet peppers.**

Drain potatoes, cut into ¾-in. (2-cm) cubes and stir into dressing while still hot.

Refrigerate until cold. Then stir in more oil if needed. *Serves 8 to 10.*

LIGHT LEMON & DILL POTATO SALAD

Cook **8** unpeeled potatoes in boiling water until tender, about 25 min.

Whisk I **cup light sour cream** with finely grated peel of I **lemon,** I **tbsp** freshly squeezed **lemon juice, 3 tbsp each** finely chopped **fresh dill** and **chives** or **green onions** and generous pinches of salt and pepper.

Cut cooked hot potatoes into ¼-in. (0.5-cm) slices. Overlap on a serving platter. Drizzle with sour cream mixture.

Sprinkle with chopped **fresh dill** and **chives.** *Serves 8 to 10.*

SOPHISTICATED POTATO SALAD

Cook **6** halved peeled medium potatoes
in boiling water until tender, about
25 min. Do not overcook.

Whisk **¾ cup mayonnaise** with
I tbsp horseradish, I tbsp Dijon and
pinch of pepper.

Add **I** chopped red pepper, **I** finely chopped
celery stalk, including leaves, and
½ small red onion, sliced into rings.

Drain potatoes, cut into bite-size pieces
and stir into mayonnaise mixture. Fold
together until blended. Refrigerate until
cooled. *Serves 4 to 6.*

SUPER FAST DILLED POTATO SALAD

Combine **2** hot cubed cooked potatoes
with **¼ cup** bottled cucumber dressing
and **2 tbsp** chopped fresh dill. *Serves 2.*

OLD-FASHIONED POTATO SALAD

Combine **8** cubed cooked hot potatoes
with **2** chopped hard-boiled eggs,
I½ cups thinly sliced celery,
½ cup chopped green onions,
¼ cup thinly sliced radishes and
¼ cup chopped gherkins or sweet pickles.

Stir **I½ cups mayonnaise** with **3 tbsp** sweet
pickle juice, **I tbsp** regular prepared
mustard, **I tsp** salt and pinch of pepper.

Stir with potatoes. *Serves 8 to 10.*

OLD-FASHIONED POTATO SALAD

R is for Rice . . . .

*SPRING VEGETABLE LEMON RISOTTO (see recipe page 90) is
a refreshing yet creamy and comforting meal. A few stirs
is all it takes to make this one-dish microwave entrée.*

RICE

*Rice is deservedly the most popular grain in the world.
Valued for its B vitamins, rice is moving from the side of our plates to the centre, where
it is often embellished with bold spices and bits of meat and vegetables.*

SPRING VEGETABLE LEMON RISOTTO

Microwave **2 tbsp butter**, on high, 1 min.
Stir in **1½ cups short-grain rice,**
  preferably Arborio, until coated.
  Microwave, covered, 2 min.
Stir in **10-oz. can condensed chicken broth,**
  3 cups water, ⅓ cup white wine, grated
  peel and juice of **1 lemon** and **½ tsp salt.**
  Microwave, covered, on high, stirring
  twice, until rice is tender, 25 min.
Stir in **½ lb (250 g) sliced asparagus,**
  1 cup green peas and **¼ cup chopped**
  fresh basil. Microwave, covered,
  stirring once, 5 min.
Stir in **¼ to ½ cup grated Parmesan,**
  1 chopped tomato and **2 thinly sliced**
  green onions. *Serves 6.*

FRUITED BASMATI RICE

Melt **1 tbsp butter.** Stir in **1 cup rinsed**
  basmati rice, 1 tsp finely minced fresh
  ginger or **½ tsp ground ginger, ¼ tsp salt**
  and **½ tsp cinnamon.**
Add **2¼ cups chicken** or **vegetable broth,**
  ½ cup chopped dried apricots and
  ¼ cup currants or **raisins.**
Bring to a boil. Cover and simmer until all
  liquid is absorbed, from 20 to 25 min.
Let stand, covered, 5 min. Fluff and serve.
  Serves 4.

COCONUT-MANGO RICE

Heat **1½ tsp vegetable oil** with
  ¾ cup shredded sweetened coconut
  and stir until golden, 1 min.
Add **1 finely chopped onion** and cook
  for 1 min.
Stir in **2 cups long-grain rice, 4 cups chicken**
  or **vegetable broth** and **¼ tsp salt.**
  Bring to a boil. Cover and simmer until
  tender, from 20 to 25 min. Drain.
Stir in **1 chopped peeled mango** and
  ¼ cup chopped fresh coriander.
  Serves 4 to 6.

RICE TIMBALES

Bring to a boil **2 cups chicken bouillon**
  or **vegetable broth.** Stir in
  1 cup long-grain rice. Cover and
  simmer until broth is absorbed, from
  20 to 25 min.
Sauté **½ minced small red pepper** and
  ½ minced small yellow pepper in
  3 tbsp butter until soft, about 5 min.
Add **1 tsp dried leaf thyme** and **¼ tsp turmeric**
  and sauté, 1 min.
Stir into cooked rice with **½ cup grated**
  Parmesan, ¼ cup finely chopped parsley
  and **pinch of pepper.**
Preheat oven to 375°F (190°C). Press rice
  mixture into 4 (6-oz/175-mL) greased
  custard cups. Cover and bake, about
  15 min. Run a knife around edges and
  invert onto plates. *Serves 4.*

Coconut-Mango Rice

Fried Rice 'n' Peas

Bring to a boil **2 cups chicken bouillon**
or water and **1 cup long-grain rice**.

Stir in **½ tsp salt** and **¼ to ½ tsp hot red
pepper flakes**. Cover and simmer, 25 min.

Sauté **1 chopped onion** and **1 minced
garlic clove** in **2 tbsp olive oil** over
medium-high heat, 5 min.

Add rice and **¼ tsp pepper**. Sauté, stirring
and scraping up brown bottom crust,
until rice is flecked with browned bits,
about 5 min.

Gently stir in **19-oz can drained kidney beans
or black-eyed peas**. Cook until hot, 2 min.
Serves 6.

Coconut-Curry Rice

Sauté **1 finely chopped onion** sprinkled
with **½ tsp curry powder** in **1 tbsp butter**
until soft, 5 min.

Stir in **¾ cup long-grain rice**. Add
14-oz (400-mL) can coconut milk and
¼ tsp salt. Bring to a boil.

Cover and barely simmer until coconut milk
is absorbed, from 15 to 20 min.

Add salt and pepper to taste. *Serves 3 to 4.*

Whole Spice Pilaf

Sauté **1 chopped onion** and **2 minced
garlic cloves** in **2 tbsp olive oil** until soft,
about 5 min.

Stir in **1 tsp cumin seeds, 4 cardamom pods,
1 small cinnamon stick** and **2 whole cloves**.
Stir for 1 min.

Stir in **1 cup rice**. Add **2¼ cups water,
¼ tsp salt** and **2 bay leaves**. Bring to a boil.

Cover and simmer until water is absorbed,
from 20 to 25 min. Let stand, covered,
5 min. Remove bay leaves. Fluff and serve.
Serves 4.

Curried Rice with Almonds & Raisins

Sauté **1 finely chopped onion** and
2 tsp curry powder in **1 tbsp vegetable oil**.
Stir often for 5 min.

Stir in **1 cup long-grain rice**, then
2½ cups chicken or vegetable bouillon.
Cover and simmer, 15 min.

Stir in **¼ cup raisins**. Continue simmering,
covered, about 5 to 10 more min.

Sprinkle with **3 tbsp toasted slivered almonds**.
Serves 4.

A B C D E F G H I J K L M N O P Q R S T U V W X Y Z

RICE
◆ *continued* ◆

SPANISH RICE

Sauté 1 minced garlic clove and 2 finely chopped seeded jalapeños in 1 tbsp olive oil, about 3 min.

Stir in 3 chopped seeded large tomatoes and ¼ tsp each paprika, salt and pepper. Stir often for 5 min.

Add 19-oz can drained black or kidney beans (optional), 3 to 4 cups hot cooked rice, ¼ cup each sliced black and stuffed green olives and 2 sliced green onions. Stir often until hot.

Then stir in ½ cup grated mozzarella. *Serves 4.*

HEALTHY GREEK SALAD

Combine 2 cups cooked rice with 2 chopped plum tomatoes, 2 thinly sliced green onions and 2 cups chopped cucumber.

Whisk 2 tbsp olive oil with 2 tbsp freshly squeezed lemon juice, ½ tsp dried oregano and generous pinches of garlic powder, salt and pepper.

Stir into salad with ½ cup crumbled feta or goat cheese.

Serve in whole-wheat pita for lunch or over salad greens. *Serves 2.*

VEGETARIAN BURRITOS

Bring 2 cups vegetable or chicken bouillon to a boil. Stir in 1 cup long-grain rice, ½ cup salsa and ¼ tsp hot red pepper flakes (optional). Cover and simmer, stirring occasionally until rice is almost tender, 20 min.

Stir in 1 cup corn kernels and 19-oz can drained Romano or kidney beans. Cook, stirring often, until hot, about 5 min.

Stir in 1 to 2 cups grated cheese.

Spoon down centre of 8 to 10 large tortillas.

Top with salsa, chopped fresh tomatoes, light sour cream, fresh coriander or shredded lettuce. *Serves 4 to 5.*

SNAPPY SPINACH RICE

Stir 3 cups cooked hot or cold rice with 1 cup shredded spinach, 2 tsp freshly squeezed lemon juice and 1 minced garlic clove. *Serves 3 to 4.*

LEMON-DILL RICE

Stir 3 cups cooked hot or cold rice with ¼ cup chopped fresh dill and 2 tsp freshly grated lemon peel. *Serves 3 to 4.*

*SAVORY TOASTED
PECAN RICE*

CURRIED ALMOND RICE

Stir **3** cups cooked hot rice with
    1 tsp curry powder and
    ½ cup chopped almonds. *Serves 3 to 4.*

VEGETABLE FRIED RICE

Stir-fry **1** diced red pepper in
    1½ tbsp vegetable oil, 1 min.
Add **1** lightly beaten egg and stir-fry just
    until it starts to set, about 1 min.
Add **¼** cup peas and **2** cups cooked rice and
    stir-fry until heated through, about 4 min.
Stir in **a** few dashes of soy sauce. *Serves 2.*

SAVORY TOASTED PECAN RICE

Sauté **1** chopped large onion, **4** grated carrots
    and **3** minced garlic cloves in **1** tbsp butter.
    Stir often for 5 min.
Stir in **1½** cups long-grain rice,
    3 cups chicken or vegetable broth,
    1 tsp dried leaf thyme and **½** tsp salt.
    Cover and bring to a boil. Simmer, 25 min.
Stir in **¾** cup snipped fresh chives,
    ¼ cup shredded basil leaves and
    ½ cup toasted pecan halves or
    roasted peanuts. *Serves 6.*

S is for Squash . . .

SPINACH & WATERCRESS SALAD *(see recipe page 96) is beautiful and robust. Bright orange slices add lively contrast. Perfect for a brunch or special gathering.*

A
B
C
D
E
F
G
H
I
J
K
L
M
N
O
P
Q
R
S
T
U
V
W
X
Y
Z

SPINACH

Whether fresh or in prewashed bags, nutrient-rich spinach has a lot going for it.
In midwinter, bags of spinach are one of the best buys in the produce section.
One bag holds about 7 cups, which during cooking collapses to about 2.

SPINACH & WATERCRESS SALAD

Combine **1 bag torn spinach** with
    1 bunch watercress, stems removed,
    finely grated peel of **1 orange** and
    2 thinly sliced peeled oranges.
Whisk **3 tbsp olive oil** with
    2 tbsp white vinegar, 1 to 2 tsp Dijon,
    1 tsp sugar and **¼ tsp** each salt and pepper.
Toss with salad. *Serves 4.*

ORIENTAL SPINACH SALAD

Heat **1 tbsp olive oil** with **2 tsp** each soy sauce
    and lemon juice, **1 tsp** dark sesame oil and
    ½ tsp Dijon. Whisk until evenly blended.
When hot, remove from heat. Immediately
    add **½ bag torn spinach** and toss until
    coated with dressing but not totally wilted.
Add remaining **½ bag torn spinach** and toss.
Salt to taste and serve immediately. *Serves 2.*

CHOPPED EGG 'N' SPINACH SALAD

Whisk **2 tbsp olive oil** with **1 tbsp balsamic**
    vinegar, 1 minced small garlic clove,
    ¼ tsp salt and pinches of pepper.
Toss with **1 bag torn spinach,**
    2 finely chopped hard-boiled eggs and
    3 tbsp chopped red or green onion.
    Taste and add **1 tbsp balsamic vinegar,**
    if needed.
Serve with slices of **dark pumpernickel.**
    Serves 2.

INDIAN SPICED SALAD

Heat **1 tsp butter or oil** with
    1 minced garlic clove and **¼ tsp** each
    hot red pepper flakes, curry and
    chili powder. Stir in **2 tbsp water.**
Add **1 bag torn spinach.** Toss just until
    coated. Serve immediately. *Serves 2.*

ORANGE & BLUE CHEESE SALAD

Peel and cut **2 oranges** into bite-size pieces.
Toss with **4 cups torn spinach, ¼ cup** bottled
    blue cheese or Roquefort salad dressing
    and **½ tsp** dried dillweed. *Serves 2.*

BLUE CHEESE & SPINACH SALAD

Stir **½ cup plain yogurt** with
    ½ cup crumbled blue cheese and
    2 thinly sliced green onions.
    Add freshly ground black pepper.
Combine **4 cups torn spinach** and
    3 ripe tomatoes, cut into wedges.
Drizzle with blue cheese dressing.
    Serves 3 to 4.

SPINACH & PEAR SALAD

Combine **1 bag torn spinach** with
    1 thinly sliced unpeeled pear.
Stir **2 tbsp finely chopped chutney,** preferably
    mango, with **¼ cup Italian dressing.**
Just before serving, toss with salad. *Serves 2.*

SPINACH SALAD WITH MINT

Whisk ¼ cup olive oil with
  1½ tbsp freshly squeezed lemon juice,
  ¼ cup finely chopped fresh mint or
  2 tsp crumbled dried mint,
  ¼ tsp each sugar and pepper and
  pinch of salt.
Combine 1 bag torn spinach with
  1 peeled segmented pink grapefruit
  and 2 thinly sliced green onions.
Toss with dressing. *Serves 3 to 4.*

APPLE & HONEY SPINACH SALAD

Whisk 1 tbsp olive oil with 1 tsp cider
  or balsamic vinegar, 1 tsp liquid honey and
  ½ tsp grainy mustard.
When ready to serve, stir with 4 cups torn
  spinach and 2 sliced unpeeled small apples.
  Serves 2 to 3.

CURRIED PEAS & SPINACH SALAD

Stir ¼ cup mayonnaise
  with 1 tsp curry powder.
Add 2½ cups cooked peas. Refrigerate.
Just before serving, stir in 2 cups shredded
  fresh spinach and salt to taste. *Serves 4.*

SPINACH & FRESH DILL SALAD

Whisk 3 tbsp olive oil with 2 tbsp freshly
  squeezed lemon juice and ¼ tsp salt.
  Add ½ finely chopped peeled cucumber.
Toss dressing with 1 bag torn spinach.
  Add ½ cup coarsely chopped fresh dill.
Sprinkle with **toasted cumin seeds**
  (see recipe page 116) or **walnuts** (optional).
  Serves 4.

Apple & Honey Spinach Salad

SPINACH
• *continued* •

SPINACH SALAD WITH ROASTED PEARS

Preheat oven to 425°F (220°C). Peel
4 ripe pears. Cut in half lengthwise
and core. Place cut-side down on a
buttered pie plate.

Drizzle with 1 tbsp melted butter. Crumble
1 tbsp brown sugar over top and sprinkle
with pinch of ground ginger.

Roast, uncovered, basting once with juices,
until lightly browned, about 30 min. Cool.

Whisk 1 tbsp olive oil with 1 tbsp lemon juice,
1 minced small garlic clove and pinches of
salt and pepper.

Toss with 1 bag torn spinach.

Arrange on plates and top with sliced pears
and 2 tbsp chopped toasted hazelnuts or
slivered almonds. *Serves 4.*

SPINACH & BASIL SALAD

Combine 1 bag torn spinach with
$\frac{1}{4}$ cup fresh basil leaves and
$\frac{1}{4}$ cup chopped red onion.

Add 1 peeled sliced orange. Sprinkle with
$\frac{1}{4}$ lb (125 g) cubed smoked Edam or
Gouda cheese or crumbled goat cheese
and 2 tbsp toasted pine nuts (optional).

Whisk 3 tbsp olive oil with 1 tbsp red
wine vinegar, 1 tsp brown sugar,
$\frac{1}{2}$ tsp dried oregano, $\frac{1}{4}$ tsp pepper
and pinches of salt.

Toss dressing with salad just before serving.
Serves 4.

INSTANT CREAMED SPINACH

Coarsely chop 2 bags spinach. Microwave in
an 8-cup (2-L) dish, covered, on high for
3 min. Drain well.

Stir in 2 to 4 tbsp sour cream and pinches of
nutmeg, salt and pepper. *Serves 2.*

SUMPTUOUS SHALLOT SPINACH

Sauté 1 tbsp finely chopped shallots in
1 tsp butter for 2 min.

Stir in 1 bag torn spinach, $\frac{1}{4}$ cup sour cream,
1 tsp freshly squeezed lemon juice
and generous pinch of salt.

Continue cooking, uncovered, stirring often,
just until spinach is hot. *Serves 2.*

GREEK FRITTATA

Whisk 8 eggs with $\frac{1}{4}$ tsp pepper.

Sauté 1 finely chopped small onion and
1 minced garlic clove in 1 tbsp olive oil
until softened, about 5 min.

Stir in 4 cups torn spinach until wilted, about
2 min. Crumble 1 cup feta over top.

Pour in egg mixture. Cook, stirring and
scraping pan bottom often, until eggs have
just begun to set, about 5 min.

Sprinkle with $\frac{1}{2}$ cup grated mozzarella.
Cover and continue cooking until
eggs are set, about 3 min.

Cut into wedges. *Serves 4 to 6.*

*PEA &
SPINACH
SOUP*

DIJON SPINACH

Sauté 2 minced garlic cloves in 1 tbsp butter
  for 1 min. Whisk in 2 tsp Dijon.
Add 1 bag torn spinach. Stir just until wilted.
  Serves 2.

BASIL SPINACH SOUP

Sauté 1 finely chopped onion and 2 minced
  garlic cloves in 1 tbsp olive oil until soft,
  about 5 min.
Stir in 1 bag torn spinach, 2 cups frozen peas,
  2 (10-oz) cans undiluted chicken broth and
  1 cup water or $3\frac{1}{2}$ cups vegetable broth,
  1 tbsp freshly squeezed lemon juice,
  1 tbsp dried basil and $\frac{1}{4}$ tsp pepper.
Simmer, covered, until peas are very tender,
  about 8 min. Purée until smooth.
Stir in $\frac{1}{2}$ cup half-and-half cream. *Serves 6.*

PEA & SPINACH SOUP

Simmer 2 cups peas and 2 thinly sliced
  green onions in 1 cup chicken or
  vegetable bouillon until peas are soft,
  about 5 min.
Purée until fairly smooth. Return to saucepan.
Add 2 more cups chicken or vegetable
  bouillon, 1 tsp dried basil and
  $\frac{1}{4}$ tsp white pepper. Cover and
  simmer, 5 min.
Stir in 2 cups shredded spinach and
  $\frac{1}{2}$ cup sour cream. *Serves 4.*

SQUASH

Squash has progressed from its stodgy image to star in everything from risottos to stews.
Sauté, mash or microwave with lots of hot 'n' hip seasonings.
And don't forget, it's fibre dense and loaded with vitamin A.

SPICY SQUASH SAUTÉ

Pierce a squash, about 1½ lbs (750 g).
Place in the microwave. Cook, on high,
until soft enough to cut, about 8 min.
Peel and scoop out seeds. Cut into
bite-size chunks.

Sauté 2 chopped large onions, 2 minced
garlic cloves, 1 tbsp cumin, 1 tsp ground
coriander and ¼ tsp hot red pepper flakes
in 1 tbsp olive oil for 2 min.

Stir in squash and ½ cup water. Cover and
simmer, stirring often, until squash is
tender, about 10 min. *Serves 4.*

SQUASH 'N' APPLE SOUP

Peel and seed 2 cooked acorn squashes.
Cut into chunks.

Sauté 1 finely chopped onion and
2 tsp minced fresh ginger or pinch
of ground ginger in 2 tbsp butter,
about 3 min.

Stir in 4 diced peeled apples, ¾ tsp chili
powder, ¼ tsp salt and generous pinch
of cinnamon. Cook for 2 min.

Add 4 cups chicken or vegetable broth and
squash. Bring to a boil. Simmer, covered,
until tender, about 15 to 20 min. Purée
until smooth. Return to saucepan and
heat through.

Serve with a dollop of sour cream (optional).
Serves 8.

GOLDEN SQUASH RISOTTO

Sauté 1 chopped onion and 2 minced
garlic cloves in 2 tbsp butter until
softened, 5 min.

Stir in 1½ cups short-grain rice, preferably
Arborio until coated. While constantly
stirring, add ½ cup white wine. Stir often
until wine is absorbed. Gradually add
another ½ cup white wine, again stirring
until absorbed.

Add 2 (10-oz) cans chicken broth and
1 cup water or 3½ cups vegetable broth,
adding ½ cup at a time, stirring often and
waiting until liquid is absorbed before
adding more. Stop adding when rice is
tender and sauce creamy, from 25 to 30 min.

Add 2 cups cooked puréed squash,
¼ tsp each grated nutmeg, dried leaf thyme
and cayenne pepper.

Stir in 1 cup peas. When hot, after 2 to 5 min.,
stir in ⅓ cup grated Parmesan.

Add salt to taste. Serve immediately with
extra cheese scattered over top. *Serves 4.*

HERBED SQUASH SOUP

Combine 4 cups chicken or vegetable broth,
2 (12-oz/300-g) pkg frozen puréed squash,
½ tsp dried leaf thyme, ¼ tsp white pepper
and pinches of salt and nutmeg.

Cook, covered, stirring occasionally, until
boiling. Simmer for 5 min.

Stir in 6 thinly sliced green onions and garnish
with dollops of sour cream. *Serves 8.*

QUICK ORANGE SQUASH

Combine 12-oz (300-g) pkg frozen puréed
squash with ½ tbsp undiluted orange juice
concentrate, ½ tbsp butter and generous
pinches of salt, white pepper and nutmeg.

Cook, covered, stirring often, until piping hot,
from 8 to 10 min. *Serves 4.*

EASY-TO-BAKE SQUASH

Slice 1 small acorn squash, crosswise,
into ¼-in. (0.5-cm) round slices.

Remove seeds and lay slices on 2 baking
sheets. Drizzle each with ¼ cup water
and dot with 1 tbsp butter.

Sprinkle with salt and pepper. Cover with
foil. Bake on bottom rack at 450°F (230°C)
until squash is fork-tender, about 20 min.
Serves 4.

HEARTY HARVEST STEW

Pierce the skin of 1 acorn squash. Microwave,
on high, 10 min. Peel, seed and chop squash.

Sauté 2 chopped large onions and
2 minced garlic cloves in 2 tbsp olive oil,
until softened, about 5 min.

Add 28-oz can undrained diced tomatoes,
4 cups chicken or vegetable broth,
19-oz can drained black beans,
2 tbsp chopped jalapeños, 2 tsp cumin,
1 tsp ground coriander, generous pinches
of salt and cayenne and squash. Bring to
a boil. Cover and simmer, 20 min.

Add 2 sliced zucchini. Sprinkle with
chopped fresh coriander or parsley.
Serves 6 to 8.

HEARTY HARVEST STEW

T is for Tomatoes . . . .

ORIENTAL TOMATO SALAD *(see recipe page 104)*
looks to the East for flavor. Sesame oil, fresh lime
juice and ginger add to its intriguing dressing.

T

TOMATOES

*Few tastes quite compare with the sweet tang of vine-ripened
tomatoes freshly sliced. But au naturel isn't the only way.
From fried green tomatoes to luscious appetizers, here's a bushel of recipe ideas.*

ORIENTAL TOMATO SALAD

Cover a platter with **4 cups mixed greens.**
   Slice **4 ripe tomatoes.** Overlap on greens.
Whisk **2 tbsp vegetable oil** with
   **2 tsp sesame oil, 3 tbsp rice wine
   vinegar** or **2 tbsp lime juice,**
   1 minced garlic clove,
   1 tsp minced fresh ginger,
   **¼ tsp each hot red pepper flakes,
   salt** and **sugar.** Drizzle over tomatoes.
Scatter with **2 sliced green onions** and
   toasted sesame seeds. *Serves 4.*

NOUVELLE SCALLOPED TOMATOES

Preheat oven to 450°F (230°C). Sauté
   3 minced garlic cloves in **1 tbsp olive oil**
   for 1 min. Add **3 cups dry bread cubes**
   and brown, 3 min.
Turn into buttered 10-inch (25-cm) pie plate.
   Sprinkle with **½ cup grated Parmesan.**
Add **3 chopped seeded large tomatoes** to
   hot pan. Cook, uncovered and stirring
   often, until thickened, 5 min.
Stir in **¼ cup chopped fresh basil** or
   1 tbsp dried basil and **¼ tsp salt.**
Pour over bread cubes. Sprinkle with
   2 cups grated provolone or **mozzarella.**
Bake until golden, about 10 min. *Serves 4 to 6.*

GREAT GAZPACHO

Coarsely chop **6 large tomatoes,**
   **½ English cucumber, ½ onion, 1 sweet
   red pepper** and **2 seeded jalapeños.**
Combine in a food processor with
   **1 tbsp olive oil, 2 tbsp red wine vinegar,
   2 minced garlic cloves, ½ tsp each salt,
   celery salt** and **dried oregano, ¼ tsp each
   hot pepper sauce** and **Worcestershire** and
   4 large basil leaves or **½ tsp dried basil.**
Whirl until finely chopped. Refrigerate until
   cold. *Serves 6.*

SICILIAN PASTA

Cook **½ lb (250 g) fettuccine** or **linguine**
   in boiling salted water until al dente,
   about 8 min.
Sauté **1 finely chopped onion** and **1 minced
   garlic clove** in **¼ cup olive oil** until onion
   has softened, about 5 min.
Add **2 cups halved ripe cherry tomatoes** or
   2 coarsely chopped large tomatoes,
   ½ cup chopped fresh basil or **1 tbsp dried
   basil, ½ tsp salt** and **pinch of pepper.**
   Stir occasionally, until hot, about 3 min.
Toss with drained pasta. Sprinkle with grated
   Parmesan. *Serves 4.*

TOMATO-CUCUMBER SALAD

In a small bowl, whisk 2 tbsp vegetable or olive oil with 2 tbsp red wine vinegar, 1 tsp dried basil, $\frac{1}{2}$ tsp dried oregano and generous pinches of thyme, salt and pepper.

Stir in 4 coarsely chopped seeded ripe tomatoes and 1 chopped peeled small cucumber. *Serves 4.*

STUFFED TOMATOES

In a large frying pan, sauté $\frac{1}{4}$ cup finely chopped green pepper in 1 tbsp olive oil for 2 min.

Stir in 1 cup cooked rice, $\frac{1}{3}$ cup cooked or canned black beans, 1 sliced green onion and $\frac{1}{4}$ tsp each dried basil, salt and pepper. Stir often until hot.

Meanwhile, slice ½-in. (1-cm) thick piece off tops of 4 large tomatoes. Scoop out pulp, discarding seeds and juice. Coarsely chop and stir into rice in pan.

Spoon into tomato shells and serve. *Serves 4.*

SPICY MICROWAVE TOMATO SOUP

Combine 2 tbsp olive oil, 1 large chopped onion, 2 tbsp finely chopped jalapeño and 3 minced garlic cloves. Microwave, covered, on high, 3 min.

Stir in 28-oz can diced tomatoes, including juice, 10-oz can undiluted chicken broth or 1 cup vegetable broth, 1 tsp granulated sugar and $\frac{1}{2}$ tsp each cumin and pepper.

Microwave, covered, on high, until hot, from 15 to 20 min. Stir once.

Stir in $\frac{1}{2}$ cup chopped parsley. *Serves 4.*

Stuffed Tomatoes

TOMATOES
◆ continued ◆

GREEK LEMON TOMATOES

Whisk ¼ cup creamy feta dressing
 with 2 tsp freshly squeezed lemon juice,
 1 finely chopped green onion and
 ¼ tsp each salt and pepper.
Slice 4 ripe tomatoes and drizzle with
 dressing. *Serves 4.*

TOMATO & BASIL TOPPER

Stir 1 tbsp olive oil with 1 minced garlic clove,
 1 tsp balsamic vinegar and ¼ tsp each salt
 and pepper.
Stir in 2 tbsp finely chopped fresh basil
 and 2 coarsely chopped drained
 large tomatoes.
Great with Eggplant Steaks (see recipe
 page 41). *Makes 1½ cups.*

HARVEST TOMATO CHÈVRE SALAD

In a small bowl, whisk 2 tbsp olive oil
 with 1 tbsp balsamic vinegar,
 1 minced large garlic clove and
 ¼ tsp each salt and pepper.
Add 6 to 8 chopped tomatoes,
 1 thinly sliced red onion and
 1 finely chopped seeded jalapeño.
Toss gently and stir in ¼ cup shredded
 fresh basil.
Serve on lettuce sprinkled with
 ¼ to ½ cup chèvre. *Serves 4.*

CHUNKY FRESH TOMATO SOUP

Blanch 6 lbs (3 kg) ripe tomatoes, about
 18 medium tomatoes, in boiling water for
 2 min. Peel, seed and finely chop.
Sauté 1 chopped onion with 1 chopped
 sweet pepper and 2 minced garlic cloves
 in 2 tbsp olive oil, 5 min.
Stir in 2 tbsp tomato paste and stir for
 1 min. Stir in chopped tomatoes and
 2 tbsp chopped fresh basil or 1 tsp dried
 basil, 1 tbsp chopped fresh thyme or
 ½ tsp dried leaf thyme and ¼ tsp each salt
 and pepper. Bring to a boil. Cover and
 simmer, stirring occasionally, 30 min.
Stir in 1 cup chicken or vegetable broth or
 ½ cup white wine. *Serves 8 to 10.*

TOMATO & FRESH BEAN TOSS

Cook ½ lb (250 g) trimmed green or yellow
 beans in boiling water until tender-crisp,
 3 min. Drain and cool. Diagonally slice
 into 1-in. (2.5-cm) pieces.
Combine with 8 coarsely chopped seeded
 plum tomatoes.
Whisk 2 tbsp olive oil with 2 tbsp sherry or
 cider vinegar, 1½ tsp Dijon, 1 tsp finely
 chopped fresh tarragon or ¼ tsp dried
 tarragon and ¼ tsp salt. Toss with salad.
Serve on a bed of arugula. Scatter with
 ¼ cup toasted pine nuts. *Serves 4.*

HERBED TOMATO TOSS

Combine 6 coarsely chopped tomatoes with
1 chopped avocado, 2 cups sliced celery
and 2 tbsp chopped fresh chives or
2 thinly sliced green onions.

Whisk ½ cup bottled Italian dressing
with 1 tsp dried oregano and
¼ tsp dried leaf thyme.

Toss with vegetables. *Serves 6 to 8.*

TOMATO & BASIL SALAD

Overlap 3 to 4 sliced large ripe tomatoes
on a serving dish. Grind lots of black
pepper over top and add a generous
sprinkling of sugar.

Whisk 2 tbsp olive oil with 1 tbsp white wine
vinegar. Drizzle over tomatoes.

Just before serving, scatter with
2 tbsp shredded fresh basil. *Serves 4.*

FRIED GREEN TOMATOES

Place ¼ cup all-purpose flour and
generous pinches of salt and cayenne
in a shallow bowl.

Cut 2 large green tomatoes into
½-in. (1-cm) slices. Coat a tomato slice
in flour. Shake off excess and slide into
1 tbsp melted butter in hot frying pan.
Repeat with 3 more slices.

When browned, about 4 min., sprinkle tops
with 1 tbsp brown sugar. Turn and fry
until caramelized, about 4 min. Add more
butter if needed.

Sprinkle with 1 tbsp brown sugar, turn and
cook until both sides are caramelized,
about 2 min. Repeat with remaining slices.
Serves 4.

FRIED GREEN TOMATOES

TOMATOES
• continued •

BALSAMIC TOMATOES

Whisk 2 tbsp balsamic vinegar with
1 minced garlic clove,
1/4 tsp granulated sugar and
pinches of salt and pepper.
Slice 4 ripe tomatoes and drizzle
with dressing.
Sprinkle with chopped fresh parsley
or green onion. *Serves 4.*

CHÈVRE-CORIANDER TOMATOES

Preheat oven to 450°F (230°C). In a food
processor, whirl 1/2 cup chèvre with
1 seeded jalapeño, 1/2 cup coriander leaves
and 1/4 tsp each salt and cumin until smooth.
Stir in 1 cup fine fresh bread crumbs
or 1/2 cup dry bread crumbs.
Slice 4 ripe tomatoes and top with dressing.
Bake on lowest rack in preheated oven
until topping is golden, from 7 to 10 min.
Serves 4.

GREEN BEANS & TOMATO SALAD

Cook 1 1/2 lbs (750 g) trimmed green beans
in boiling water until tender-crisp,
3 min. Drain.
Combine with 2 seeded chopped
small tomatoes and 1 thinly sliced
small red onion.
Whisk 1/4 cup olive oil with
1 to 2 tbsp freshly squeezed lemon juice,
1 tsp Dijon, 1 minced garlic clove and
pinches of salt and pepper. Pour over
vegetables and toss. *Serves 6.*

GREEN PEPPER & TOMATO APPETIZER

Combine 1 chopped green pepper with
1 chopped small sweet onion. Sprinkle
over 4 sliced tomatoes.
Stir 2 tbsp olive oil with 1 to 2 tbsp balsamic
vinegar, 1 minced garlic clove, 1/2 tsp salt
and 1/4 tsp pepper. Drizzle over tomatoes.
Serves 4.

CURRIED SQUASH & TOMATOES

Heat 1 tbsp butter with 1/4 cup water,
1 thinly sliced onion, 2 minced garlic cloves
and 1 tbsp curry powder.
Cook, stirring often, until water has
evaporated, about 2 min.
Stir in 4 cups bite-size pieces squash,
2 coarsely chopped large tomatoes with
juice and seeds and 1/4 tsp salt.
Cook, covered, stirring often, 15 min.
Add 1 chopped large green pepper.
Cook for 5 more min. *Serves 4.*

GINGER-SOY TOMATOES

Whisk 2 tbsp rice wine vinegar with
2 tsp each dark sesame oil and soy sauce,
1 tbsp minced fresh ginger,
2 tsp granulated sugar and
1 minced large garlic clove.
Thickly slice 4 ripe tomatoes and drizzle
with dressing. *Serves 4.*

Vibrant Skillet Ratatouille

OVEN-CHARRED TOMATOES

Preheat oven to 400°F (200°C). Wash,
  dry and remove hulls from
  4 cups cherry tomatoes. Place in
  9-in. (2.5-L) baking dish.
Stir 2 tbsp olive oil with 4 minced garlic cloves,
  ¼ to ½ tsp hot red pepper flakes
  and ¼ tsp salt. Pour over tomatoes and
  stir until evenly coated.
Roast, uncovered, stirring occasionally,
  until lightly charred, from 30 to 35 min.
  Serve with pilaf, roasted lamb or beef.
  Serves 4.

VIBRANT SKILLET RATATOUILLE

Sauté 1 coarsely chopped onion with
  4 minced garlic cloves in 1 tbsp olive oil
  until onion has softened, about 5 min.
Stir in 4 to 6 coarsely chopped tomatoes,
  including juice, 2 chopped sweet peppers,
  2 cups corn kernels, 1 tsp granulated sugar
  and ½ tsp each cumin and salt. Bring to a
  boil, then simmer, uncovered, 10 min.
Stir in 2 julienned zucchini and continue
  cooking, stirring often, until vegetables are
  hot, about 2 min.
Toss with pasta or spoon on rice and sprinkle
  with chopped fresh basil. *Serves 8.*

TORTILLAS

Tortillas have rolled way beyond white rounds to now sport fashionable pastel hues, colorful vegetable flecks and flavors from banana to sun-dried tomato. For a light supper, bypass bread and just roll up your favorite sandwich fixings in a tortilla or make a vegetarian lasagna.

MICROWAVE MEXICAN LASAGNA

Stir 1½ cups salsa with 1 cup spaghetti sauce and ¼ tsp hot red pepper flakes (optional). Spread a thin layer in bottom of a 9-in. (23-cm) microwave dish.

Mix 16-oz (475-g) container ricotta cheese with 1 beaten egg.

Cut 9 small tortillas in half. Lay 6 halves over sauce, overlapping as needed. Spread with half of ricotta mixture.

Chop 1 green pepper and ½ cup onion and sprinkle half over ricotta. Drizzle with ½ cup sauce and sprinkle with ½ cup grated Monterey Jack or mozzarella. Repeat, ending with tortillas. Cover with remaining sauce.

Microwave, covered, on medium, until centre is hot, from 25 to 35 min.

Sprinkle with 1½ cups grated Monterey Jack or mozzarella and microwave, uncovered, until melted, about 1½ min. *Serves 6.*

HONEY-CRUNCH NIBBLES

Preheat oven to 350°F (180°C). Thickly brush 1 tbsp warm honey over top of 2 large plain or flavored tortillas such as banana or cinnamon-apple. Sprinkle with pinches of cinnamon.

Cut each into 8 wedges. Bake in single layer on an ungreased baking sheet until crisp, from 8 to 10 min. *Makes 16 pieces.*

TEX-MEX QUESADILLA

Over half of 1 large tortilla, sprinkle 2 tbsp drained finely chopped seeded tomatoes, ½ cup grated cheddar or Monterey Jack and 2 tbsp chopped fresh coriander or thinly sliced green onions. Fold in half. Lightly butter the outside.

In a large frying pan over medium heat, cook folded tortilla until golden, 1 to 2 min. per side. For appetizers, slice into 4 wedges. These can also be heated on the barbecue. *Makes 4 appetizers or 1 serving.*

THAI QUESADILLA

Over half of 1 large tortilla, spread 2 to 3 tbsp light cream cheese, ¼ to ½ tsp hot garlic-chili or hot pepper sauce and 2 tsp chopped fresh coriander or thinly sliced green onion. Fold in half. Brush outside with a few drops of sesame oil.

In a large frying pan over medium heat, cook folded tortilla until golden, 1 to 2 min. per side. For appetizers, slice into 4 wedges. *Makes 4 appetizers or 1 serving.*

CREAMY CHÈVRE QUESADILLA

Spread 3 tbsp creamy chèvre over 1 large tortilla. Sprinkle with 2 tbsp finely chopped avocado, 2 tbsp thinly sliced green onions and pinch of pepper. Add chopped tomato (optional). Fold in half. Gently press down and slice into 4 wedges. *Makes 4 appetizers or 1 serving.*

TORTILLA COOKIES

Preheat oven to 325°F (160°C). Spread
1 large tortilla with 2 tbsp butter.
Sprinkle with 2 tbsp brown sugar,
½ tsp cinnamon and 2 tbsp finely
chopped pecans.

Roll up tightly, then slice into ½-in. (1-cm)
rounds. Lay cut-side down on a foil-lined
baking sheet. Place rounds so they
are touching and ends cannot unroll
during baking.

Bake in centre of oven until golden, about
15 min. *Makes 10 cookies.*

ROLLED FRESH VEGETABLE SANDWICH

Spread large flour tortilla with
creamy chèvre or cream cheese.

In rows, place 2 to 3 tbsp each shredded
fresh spinach, grated carrot, paper-thin
slices of onion and chopped red pepper
or tomato.

Sprinkle with chopped fresh herbs.
Add pinches of pepper and salt and
a squeeze of lemon juice.

Snugly roll up. *Makes 1 sandwich.*

ROLLED FRESH VEGETABLE SANDWICH

X is for Xtras . . .

Curry gives a dynamite boost to harvest vegetables.
COLORFUL CAULIFLOWER CURRY *(see recipe*
page 114) bursts with fibre and flavor.

XTRAS

*Make appealing side dishes and starters with this
gathering of vegetables and fruit.*

AVOCADOS

LIME AVOCADO DIP

Mash 1 ripe avocado.

Stir in ½ cup sour cream, 1 minced garlic
clove, finely grated peel of ½ lime,
½ tsp Dijon, ¼ tsp salt and dash of
hot pepper sauce.

Great with tortilla chips. *Makes 1 cup.*

GUACAMOLE

In a food processor, whirl 1 large ripe avocado,
1 small minced garlic clove,
2 tbsp freshly squeezed lime juice,
2 chopped green onions, dash of hot
red pepper sauce and pinches of salt and
white pepper until smooth. Taste and add
more seasonings if desired.

Sprinkle with 1 chopped seeded drained
ripe tomato (optional). *Serves 4.*

BRUSSELS SPROUTS

LEMONY BRUSSELS SPROUTS

Trim away tough stem ends and cut an "X"
into base of 1½ lbs (750 g) brussels
sprouts. Cook in gently boiling water until
almost tender, about 5 min.

Sauté 1 red onion, sliced into thin rings, in
1 tbsp butter until softened, about 5 min.

Add drained sprouts, 1 tbsp freshly squeezed
lemon juice and ¼ tsp each salt and pepper.
Serves 6.

BRUSSELS SPROUTS WITH WATER CHESTNUTS

Trim away tough stem ends and cut an "X"
into base of 1 lb (500 g) brussels sprouts.
Cook in gently boiling water until almost
tender, about 5 min. Drain well.

Add 2 tbsp butter, pinch of sugar,
½ tsp whole marjoram or thyme,
salt and pepper to taste and
10-oz can sliced drained water chestnuts.
Sauté until sprouts are glazed.

Drizzle with freshly squeezed lemon juice
(optional). *Serves 4.*

CAULIFLOWER

COLORFUL CAULIFLOWER CURRY

Sauté 1 chopped onion and 2 minced garlic
cloves in 1 tbsp vegetable oil until
softened, about 5 min.

Add 2 tbsp each curry powder and
all-purpose flour. Stir constantly for 2 min.

Stir in 2 cups apple juice or water. Stir often,
until mixture begins to thicken, 4 min.

Stir in 1 cauliflower, cut into florets, and
3 peeled cubed potatoes. Cover and bring
to a boil. Simmer, stirring often, 15 min.

Add 2 chopped large tomatoes, 1 cup peas,
½ tsp salt and 2 tbsp freshly squeezed
lemon juice. Simmer until hot, 5 min.

Serve with steamed rice and Cooling Cucumber
Raita (see recipe page 116). *Serves 4.*

A B C D E F G H I J K L M N O P Q R S T U V W X Y Z

NEW-STYLE CAULIFLOWER AU GRATIN

NEW-STYLE CAULIFLOWER AU GRATIN

Cook 1 thinly sliced onion and 1 large
  minced garlic clove in 1 tbsp olive oil
  until softened, about 3 min.
Add **28-oz** can drained diced tomatoes,
  ½ tsp Italian seasonings and ¼ tsp pepper.
When bubbly, add 1 small cauliflower, cut
  into bite-size pieces. Cook, covered and
  stirring occasionally, until cauliflower is
  almost cooked, from 8 to 10 min.
Preheat broiler. Spoon mixture, including
  juice, into an 8-in. (2-L) baking dish.
Sprinkle with ½ cup each crumbled feta and
  grated mozzarella or Swiss cheese. Broil
  until golden, from 6 to 8 min.
Sprinkle with ¼ cup finely chopped fresh
  parsley. *Serves 2 to 3.*

CELERY

CELERY VICHYSSOISE

Sauté 1 chopped large onion in 1 tbsp butter
  until softened, 5 min.
Stir in **1** tbsp all-purpose flour.
Stir in **3** cups chicken or vegetable bouillon
  and freshly ground black pepper.
Add **2** cubed peeled potatoes and
  1 bunch sliced celery, about 6 cups.
Bring to a boil. Cover and simmer, from
  20 to 25 min.
Purée in a food processor. Reheat with
  1 cup milk. *Serves 4 to 6.*

XTRAS
• continued •

TOASTED PECAN, CELERY & APPLE SALAD

Toss 4 thinly sliced green apples with
  2 tbsp freshly squeezed lemon juice,
  1½ cups thinly sliced celery and
  ½ cup toasted pecan halves.
Blend 1 cup mayonnaise with
  ¼ tsp cinnamon and ⅛ tsp nutmeg.
Toss with salad. *Serves 8.*

CUCUMBER

COOLING CUCUMBER RAITA

Line a sieve with cheesecloth or large
  coffee filter and place over a bowl. Pour
  2 cups plain yogurt into cloth. Cover
  and let stand at room temperature for
  30 min. or in the refrigerator overnight.
  Discard liquid that drains off.
Stir thickened yogurt with ¼ grated unpeeled
  English cucumber with juices squeezed out,
  1 tsp freshly grated lemon peel,
  ¼ tsp salt and ½ tsp toasted cumin seeds
  (see recipe below). *Makes 1½ cups.*

TOASTED CUMIN SEEDS

Spread 2 tsp cumin seeds in a single layer
  in a dry frying pan over medium heat.
  Stir often, until seeds are fragrant and
  slightly darkened, about 4 min. Watch
  carefully to avoid burning.
Store seeds in a sealed container in the
  refrigerator for several weeks.

THAI CUCUMBER SALAD

Combine 2 tbsp each boiling water and
  granulated sugar until dissolved. Stir in
  2 tbsp white vinegar, ½ tsp hot chili paste
  and ¼ tsp salt.
Pour over ½ thinly sliced English cucumber.
  Serves 3.

FIDDLEHEADS

LEMON FIDDLEHEADS

Remove brown sheaths from
  ½ lb (250 g) fresh fiddleheads. Soak in
  several changes of cold water. Drain.
Sauté in 1 tbsp olive oil over medium-high
  heat, until tender-crisp, from 3 to 5 min.
Toss with 1 to 2 tbsp freshly squeezed lemon
  juice, 2 tbsp toasted pine nuts and
  pinches of salt and pepper. *Serves 4.*

KOHLRABI

KOHLRABI SLAW

Stir 1 cup mayonnaise or ½ cup sour cream
  and ½ cup mayonnaise with 1 tsp Dijon
  and 2 tbsp finely chopped fresh dill or
  1 tsp dried dillweed.
Trim, peel and grate 2 lbs (1 kg) kohlrabi.
Add to the dressing with 3 grated large
  carrots. Refrigerate.
Slaw is best served the same day it is made.
  Serves 6.

MANGO

MAGNIFICENT MANGO SALAD

Combine 3 julienned peeled mangoes
with 1 julienned red pepper,
1/4 cup finely chopped red onion,
1 cup chopped coriander and
1/2 cup chopped mint.
Whisk 3 tbsp lime juice with 2 tbsp fish sauce
(optional), 2 tbsp granulated sugar,
1 tsp hot red pepper flakes and 1/4 tsp salt.
Toss with salad. *Serves 4 to 6.*

PARSNIPS

PARSNIP & CARROT SOUP

Sauté 2 chopped onions and 1 minced
garlic clove in 2 tbsp butter, 5 min.
Stir in 3 shredded carrots,
3 shredded parsnips and
2 tbsp all-purpose flour.
Slowly stir in 4 cups chicken or
vegetable broth, 1/2 tsp dried leaf thyme
and 1/8 tsp curry powder.
Bring to a boil. Cover and simmer until
vegetables are very soft, from 15 to 20 min.
Stir in 2 tbsp chopped fresh dill.
Add salt and pepper to taste. Sprinkle
with grated Parmesan. *Serves 4.*

Parsnip & Carrot Soup

ABCDEFGHIJKLMNOPQRSTUVWXYZ

XTRAS
◆ continued ◆

HOLIDAY PARSNIP PURÉE

In a large covered saucepan, bring to a boil
3 lbs (1.5 kg) halved peeled parsnips. Boil
gently, partially covered, until very tender,
from 15 to 20 min.
Drain and purée. Stir in 3 tbsp butter and
1/4 tsp each nutmeg, salt and white pepper.
Serves 6 to 8.

MICROWAVE DIJON PARSNIPS

Peel and slice 1 lb (500 g) parsnips. Place in
a microwave-safe bowl with 1/4 cup water.
Microwave, covered, on high, stirring
partway through, until fork-tender,
about 5 min.
Combine 1 tbsp butter with 1/2 tsp Dijon
and generous pinches of nutmeg, salt and
pepper. Toss with drained parsnips.
Serves 4.

PEARS

CURRIED PEARS

Heat 1 tbsp butter over medium heat.
When bubbly, add 2 peeled sliced pears.
Sprinkle with 1/2 tsp each curry powder
and cumin. Sauté, stirring and turning
often, until pears are tender, from
8 to 10 min.
Add 1 tbsp marmalade or brown sugar and
toss until glazed. Serve with grains,
chicken or pork. *Serves 2.*

PEAR CHUTNEY

Sauté 1 chopped small onion in
2 tsp butter until lightly golden,
about 8 min.
Stir in 2 coarsely chopped peeled pears,
1 chopped red pepper,
2 tbsp each brown sugar and cider vinegar
and 1/4 tsp hot red pepper flakes.
Stir often until thickened, about 10 min.
Stir in 1 thinly sliced green onion.
Makes 2 cups.

PEAS

MINT-SHALLOT PEAS

Cook 3 cups frozen peas and 1/2 cup chopped
fresh mint in boiling salted water.
Cover and simmer until peas are tender,
from 3 to 5 min.
Drain and toss with 1 tbsp each butter and
shallot vinegar or white vinegar. Season
with salt and pepper. *Serves 6 to 8.*

MICROWAVE SUGAR SNAP PEAS & CASHEWS

Microwave 1 cup cashews, uncovered, on
high until lightly toasted, about 3 min.
Stir occasionally. Cool.
Combine 1 tsp butter, 1 tbsp water and
1 lb (500 g) sugar snap peas or snow peas.
Microwave, covered, stirring once, on high
until peas are tender, from 2 to 3 min. Drain.
Toss with cashews and pinches of salt. *Serves 4.*

WARM CURRIED PEA SALAD

Sauté 2 coarsely chopped onions with ½ tsp curry powder, 1 tsp cumin and generous pinch of cayenne pepper in 2 tbsp butter, 5 min.

Add 3 cups peas and 2 tbsp water. Cook, stirring often, just until peas are tender and liquid is evaporated.

Remove from heat. Stir in ½ cup sour cream.

Sprinkle with ½ cup peanuts. Serve hot or cold. *Serves 6.*

PUMPKIN

CURRIED PUMPKIN SOUP

Sauté 1 finely chopped onion with 2 minced garlic cloves, 1 tbsp curry powder and 1 tsp cumin in 1 tbsp butter until onion is soft, about 5 min.

Stir in 4 chopped peeled apples, 14-oz can pumpkin purée (not pie filling), 4 cups chicken or vegetable broth, 1 cup water and 1 tsp granulated sugar.

Bring to a boil, stirring often. Cover and simmer, stirring occasionally, for 25 min. Purée and reheat.

Swirl a little sour cream or yogurt in centre of each bowl. *Serves 6.*

CURRIED PUMPKIN SOUP

XTRAS
◆ *continued* ◆

RAPINI

RAPINI & FETA PASTA

Cook ½ (I-lb/450-g) box penne or small shell pasta in boiling salted water until al dente, about 10 min. Toss I chopped bunch rapini into boiling pasta water about 5 min. before pasta is done. Drain together.

Sauté I thinly sliced onion, I thinly sliced red pepper, I minced large garlic clove and ¼ tsp each dried basil and pepper in 3 tbsp olive oil, from 8 to 10 min.

Toss with hot drained pasta and rapini and I cup crumbled feta cheese. *Serves 4.*

SWEET POTATOES

SWEET POTATO BUFFALO FRIES

Preheat oven to 425°F (220°C). Peel and slice 4 sweet potatoes into 1-in. (2.5-cm) wedges. Toss with 3 tbsp olive oil.

Mix ⅛ to ¼ tsp each chili powder, cayenne and garlic salt. Sprinkle over potatoes and toss.

Roast on a baking sheet, uncovered and turning often, until golden, about 30 min. Sprinkle with salt. *Serves 4 to 6.*

CUMIN SWEET POTATO MASH

Cut 3 large sweet potatoes in half lengthwise. Microwave, cut-side down, uncovered, until softened, from 10 to 12 min.

Discard skins and mash. Stir in I tbsp butter, ½ tsp cumin and ¼ tsp each salt and dark sesame oil. *Serves 4.*

INTRIGUING SWEET POTATO SALAD

Prick 4 large sweet potatoes. Place on a paper towel in microwave. Microwave, on high, 10 to 15 min., turning potatoes partway through until just tender.

Combine 2 tbsp olive oil with finely grated peel and juice of I large orange, 2 tsp each sesame oil, brown sugar and Dijon, ½ tsp each salt and pepper and generous pinch of cayenne.

Stir in cubed peeled hot potatoes with I finely chopped small red onion, 2 thinly sliced celery stalks and ¼ cup snipped chives or chopped fresh coriander (optional). *Serves 6 to 8.*

TURNIPS

HONEYED TURNIP

Cover 3 small quartered unpeeled white turnips with water. Boil gently, uncovered, 10 min. Rinse under cold water and drain well.

Peel and slice into ½-in. (1-cm) pieces. Place in a shallow casserole dish.

Stir in ¼ cup liquid honey, 2 tbsp butter and pinches of salt and pepper.

Bake in preheated 350°F (180°C) oven, stirring frequently, about 30 min.

Stir in ½ to I cup sour cream.

Sprinkle with nutmeg. *Serves 8 to 10.*

Microwave Apple 'n' Rum Turnips

MICROWAVE APPLE 'N' RUM TURNIPS

Place 2½ lbs (1.25 kg) unpeeled turnips
in a paper towel-lined shallow dish in
microwave. Microwave, on high, 2 min.

Slice off peel. Cut into cubes. Place in a
microwave-safe bowl with ¼ cup water.
Microwave, covered, on high, stirring
occasionally, until soft, about 20 min.

Drain and mash. Stir in 1 cup applesauce,
1 tbsp brown sugar and 1 to 2 tbsp rum
(optional). Add salt and pepper. *Serves 4.*

GLAZED TURNIPS

Slice 1 turnip into ⅓-in. (1-cm) thick rounds.
Cut peel from rounds and discard. Slice
rounds into bite-size sticks.

Boil gently with 2 cups apple juice,
1 tbsp unsalted butter and pinches of
salt and pepper until turnips are tender
and most of the liquid is evaporated,
about 25 min. *Serves 4.*

TURNIP WITH DILL

Peel 1 medium turnip and cut into bite-size
fingers. Cover with boiling water.

Add ¼ tsp salt and 1 tbsp granulated sugar.

Simmer, partially covered, until fork-tender,
from 10 to 15 min. Drain well, but leave in
saucepan.

Add 1 tbsp butter. Sprinkle with
1 tbsp white vinegar,
1 tbsp granulated sugar, 2 tbsp chopped
fresh dill or ½ tsp dried dillweed and
pinches of salt and white pepper.

Stir over medium heat until turnip is lightly
glazed, about 2 min. *Serves 4.*

Z is for Zucchini . . .

Latkes, traditionally served during Hanukkah,
make an irresistible yet inexpensive party favorite any
time of the year. These Zucchini & Carrot Latkes
(see recipe page 124) add a new twist to an old favorite.

A
B
C
D
E
F
G
H
I
J
K
L
M
N
O
P
Q
R
S
T
U
V
W
X
Y
Z

ZUCCHINI

Zucchini is a modest veggie that lets other tastes shine through — be it garlic, lemon or Italian seasonings. Here are zippy ways to add bursts of taste to this popular vegetable.

ZUCCHINI & CARROT LATKES

Stir 2 grated zucchini with 1 tsp salt and drain.

Stir 1 beaten egg with 2 grated peeled carrots, 1/2 grated onion and 1 minced garlic clove.

When zucchini has drained 15 min., scoop up handfuls and squeeze dry. Stir into carrot mixture. Stir in 1/2 cup all-purpose flour, 1/4 tsp salt and pinch of pepper.

Heat 1 tbsp vegetable oil in a large frying pan over medium-high heat. Fill a 1/4-cup measure with vegetable mixture. Turn into hot oil. With a fork, spread into a 3-in. (7.5-cm) round with uneven edges. Repeat, adding 3 more latkes.

Cook until golden, about 2 min. per side. Repeat, adding 1 more tbsp oil to pan. *Makes 8 latkes.*

GARDEN GARLIC RELISH

Grate 1 medium-size zucchini. Place in a bowl.

Stir in 1/4 cup mayonnaise with 1 minced garlic clove, 2 tbsp finely chopped fresh dill and pinches of salt and pepper.

Serve immediately with eggs, grilled fish or chicken. *Makes 1/2 cup.*

SAUTÉED ZUCCHINI

Sauté 1/4 cup coarsely chopped almonds in 1 tsp each butter and olive oil until golden, from 2 to 3 min. Remove and set aside.

Melt 1 tbsp butter. Add 2 medium-size sliced zucchini, 1 minced garlic clove and pinches of salt and pepper.

Sauté until tender, about 4 min. Sprinkle with almonds. *Serves 6.*

ZUCCHINI STIR-FRY

Sauté 4 finely chopped shallots in 2 tbsp butter until soft, about 5 min.

Add 4 medium-size sliced zucchini, 1/2 cup chopped pecans, 1/2 tsp dried basil, 1/4 tsp salt and pinch of pepper. Stir-fry about 2 min.

Toss with 1/4 cup grated Parmesan. *Serves 4.*

ZUCCHINI RAPPA

Slice 1 large unpeeled zucchini and coarsely chop 1 seeded tomato. Combine with 1/2 tsp dried basil, 1/4 tsp dried oregano and pinches of salt.

Heat 1 minced garlic clove in 1 tbsp olive oil.

Add vegetables and stir-fry until vegetables are heated through, about 4 min. *Serves 4.*

Light Zucchini Soup

LIGHT ZUCCHINI SOUP

Sauté 1 large chopped onion, 1 minced
   garlic clove, 2 tsp curry powder and
   ½ tsp cumin (optional) in 2 tbsp butter,
   about 5 min.

Add 4 chopped medium-size zucchini,
   ½ tsp finely grated lemon peel and
   3 cups chicken or vegetable broth.

Bring to a boil. Cover and simmer, until
   zucchini is tender, 10 min. Drain zucchini
   and reserve broth.

Purée vegetables and stir back into broth.
   Heat until hot.

Crumble Stilton over each serving. *Serves 6.*

FIERY ZUCCHINI & TOMATO

Sauté ¼ to ½ tsp hot red pepper flakes and
   1 minced garlic clove in 1 tbsp olive oil,
   2 min.

Stir in 28-oz can diced tomatoes, including
   juice, ½ tsp each dried basil and oregano
   and generous pinches of salt and pepper.

Bring to a boil. Simmer, uncovered, stirring
   occasionally, for 10 min.

Add 2 chopped large zucchini. Cook until
   zucchini is hot, about 3 more min.

Sprinkle with grated Parmesan. *Serves 4.*

ZUCCHINI
◆ *continued* ◆

CURRIED GREENS WITH PASTA

Cook ½ lb (250 g) fettuccine or spaghetti
in boiling salted water until al dente,
about 8 min.

Sauté 4 minced garlic cloves in 1 tbsp butter,
about 1 min.

Add 6 coarsely chopped large tomatoes,
including juice, ½ to 1 tsp curry paste,
½ tsp salt and ½ to 1 tsp granulated sugar
(optional).

Boil gently, uncovered, until most of liquid
evaporates, about 5 min.

Stir in 3 julienned small zucchini and
1 bag torn spinach. Stir often, uncovered,
until cooked, about 3 min.

Stir in ½ cup coconut milk and
½ cup chopped fresh coriander.

Toss with drained pasta. *Serves 4.*

CORN, RED PEPPER & ZUCCHINI

Sauté 1 chopped onion and 2 minced
garlic cloves in 1 tbsp vegetable oil,
about 3 min.

Add 1 chopped red pepper, 1 sliced zucchini
and ½ cup corn kernels.

Sauté until hot, about 4 min.

Add pinches of salt, pepper and chopped
fresh coriander or parsley.

Great with eggs, burgers or chicken.
Makes 1 cup.

ITALIAN ZUCCHINI SALAD

Stir ¼ cup store-bought Italian dressing
with ½ tsp each dried basil and oregano
and pinch of pepper.

Stir in 1 lb (500 g) thinly sliced or julienned
zucchini.

Serve at room temperature with tomatoes.
Serves 4.

ZUCCHINI SALAD WITH BASIL DRESSING

Whisk ⅓ cup olive oil with 3 tbsp red
wine vinegar, 1 minced garlic clove,
1 tsp granulated sugar, ½ tsp dried oregano
and 2 tbsp finely chopped fresh basil
or 1 tsp dried basil.

Overlap 3 sliced tomatoes and 2 thinly sliced
zucchini in alternating rows.

Pour dressing over top. *Serves 4 to 6.*

TANGY ZUCCHINI PASTA SALAD

In a large bowl, whisk ½ cup olive oil with
finely grated peel of 1 lemon,
3 tbsp freshly squeezed lemon juice,
3 tbsp coarsely chopped fresh dill or basil,
½ tsp salt and pinch of pepper.

Stir in 4 cups cooked macaroni or fusilli,
1 julienned red pepper and
2 chopped zucchini. *Serves 4.*

Chocolate Zucchini Cake

Preheat oven to 350°F (180°C). Combine
  16-oz (510-g) box devil's food chocolate
  cake mix with $\frac{1}{2}$ tsp cinnamon,
  $\frac{1}{4}$ tsp ground cloves, $\frac{1}{2}$ cup buttermilk,
  $\frac{1}{3}$ cup vegetable oil and 3 eggs. Beat at low
  speed until blended.
Stir in 1 grated zucchini and 1 cup semisweet
  chocolate chips.
Pour into greased 9x13 in. (3-L) baking pan.
Sprinkle with 1 cup chopped walnuts.
Bake until a cake tester inserted in centre
  comes out clean, about 35 min. *Serves 12.*

Fall Vegetable Chowder

Cook 1 sliced onion, 2 thinly sliced celery
  stalks, 2 thinly sliced carrots and
  6 sliced mushrooms in 1 tbsp butter
  until onions are softened, about 5 min.
Add 4 to 6 chopped seeded tomatoes,
  4 cups chicken or vegetable broth,
  $\frac{1}{2}$ tsp each dried leaf thyme and oregano
  and $\frac{1}{4}$ tsp pepper. Bring to a boil.
Cover and simmer, stirring occasionally,
  until vegetables are tender, 20 to 25 min.
Add 2 sliced zucchini and pinches of salt.
  Serves 8.

Fall Vegetable Chowder

SEASONAL GUIDE

Here's all the information you need to choose, store and cook popular vegetables. They're even grouped by season so you can enjoy them when they're at their peak in flavor and texture.

SPRING

ARTICHOKES

Buying: Look for plump, compact artichokes.

Storing: Uncovered, in refrigerator crisper. Use within 3 days.

Cooking: Clean artichoke by grasping the stem and swishing in water to remove dirt between leaves. Cut off stem. Remove tough bottom leaves. Use scissors to cut off thorny tops of the leaves. To prevent discoloration, add some lemon juice or vinegar to the cooking water. To steam, place the artichoke on a rack in a pot containing 1 in. (2.5 cm) of boiling salted water. Cover and steam from 15 to 25 minutes, depending on the size of the artichoke and whether or not the choke is still intact. To simmer, submerge artichoke in boiling salted water. Cover and simmer 15 to 25 minutes. To microwave, slice ⅓ off top and trim base. Wash and leave clinging water, then wrap each in plastic wrap. Microwave on high, from 12 to 20 minutes for 4 artichokes. Enjoy by dipping tender ends of artichokes leaves and choke base in lemony vinaigrette dressing, such as Mediterranean Vinaigrette (see recipe page 62).

Nutrients: Artichokes contain potassium, calcium, phosphorus and fibre.

ASPARAGUS

Buying: Buy bright, crisp straight stalks with tight pointed tips. Choose ¼- to ½-in. (1-cm) wide equal-size spears with 1 in. (2.5 cm) or less of white at base.

Storing: Wrap stalk bottoms in damp paper towels and place in plastic bag in the refrigerator.

Cooking: Snap off woody ends. Wash stalks. Cook, stems down and covered, in 2 in. (5 cm) boiling water, from 4 to 10 minutes, depending on thickness. To microwave, arrange wagon-wheel style so tops point toward the centre of the dish. Overlap tips if necessary. Microwave, covered, on high, from 4 to 6 minutes, for 1 lb (500 g). Serve drizzled with olive oil or melted butter. Add a squeeze of lemon or drizzle of balsamic vinegar. Sprinkle with Parmesan.

Nutrients: Very rich in vitamin C. Good source of vitamin A.

BEETS

Buying: Choose smooth beets with green leaves.

Storing: Cut off the greens, leaving 1 in. (2.5 cm) stalk on the beet and trim the roots, leaving 1 in. (2.5 cm) of root on the end. Store the greens in a plastic bag in the refrigerator. Use within 2 days. Beets will keep up to 4 weeks in the refrigerator crisper.

Cooking: Scrub beets, but do not peel until after cooking. To boil, place beets in a large pot of unsalted water. Boil gently, uncovered, until barely tender, about 30 minutes. To microwave, add ¼ cup water. Microwave, on high, covered, from 15 to 20 minutes for 4 medium-size beets. To cook greens, wash and sauté without added water until wilted. Chop and toss with salt and pepper.

Nutrients: Beets are a rich source of potassium. The greens are an excellent source of beta-carotene and vitamin C.

FIDDLEHEADS

Buying: Buy tightly curled small heads.

Storing: Store in perforated plastic bag in refrigerator. Use as soon as possible.

Cooking: Trim brown ends and brush off loose paper-like husks. Wash in several changes of water. Boil or steam, from 3 to 5 minutes. To microwave, add 2 to 3 tbsp water. Microwave on high, covered, 3 to 4 minutes, for 1 lb (500 g). Toss with butter.

Nutrients: Excellent source of vitamin C.

GREEN BEANS

Buying: Fresh beans should snap when broken. Avoid large, seeded swollen pods.

Storing: Store, unwashed, in sealed plastic bags in refrigerator. Use within 5 days.

Cooking: Trim stem ends, leaving pointed ends intact, and wash. Simmer, covered, from 3 to 6 minutes. Or microwave in ¼ cup water on high, covered, 3 to 6 minutes, for ½ lb (250 g). Dab with butter. Sprinkle with chopped fresh herbs such as basil, chives or dill.

Nutrients: Reasonably good source of vitamin C. Some potassium and calcium.

SPINACH

Buying: Choose spinach with bright green leaves and an earthy aroma. If it smells like cabbage or has yellowish spots, it's past its peak.

Storing: Store in the refrigerator in a plastic bag for several days.

Cooking: Remove tough stems and wash well. Do not dry. Place wet spinach in a large pot and stir often over medium heat, just until wilted, about 3 min. Drain very well and squeeze out all liquid. To microwave, place wet spinach in a large microwave-safe bowl. Cook, covered, on high, stirring once, until spinach is just wilted, about 3 minutes for 1 large bunch, about ½ lb (250 g). Raw spinach is rich in iron, but when cooked, its oxalic acid partially blocks our bodies' ability to absorb its iron and calcium. A little vitamin C, even a squirt of lemon or orange juice, improves absorption.

Nutrients: The dark green color is an indication of spinach's powerhouse of nutrients, including vitamins A, B, C and E. As well as iron, it is also a source of dietary fibre.

SEASONAL GUIDE

SUMMER

BROCCOLI

Buying: Look for bright-colored, tight florets, firm stalks and dark leaves. Avoid thick woody stems and broccoli that gives off an odor.

Storing: Store in open plastic bag in refrigerator. Use within 3 days.

Cooking: To cook, cut off florets and slice stems. Boil, uncovered, from 4 to 5 minutes for stalks and 2 to 3 minutes for florets. To microwave, place stalks on the outside of dish as they take longer. Cover and cook on high with 2 to 3 tbsp water, from 2 to 3 minutes for a small head of broccoli.

Nutrients: Top-ranked nutritionally. Very high in vitamins A and C. Also some calcium, iron and fibre.

CARROTS

Buying: Buy firm, crisp, no blemishes or green areas. Avoid oversized.

Storing: Remove tops and store in original moisture-proof bag or plastic wrap in the refrigerator.

Cooking: Peel carrots and cut in chunks or slice. Boil gently, covered, in salted water, from 12 to 20 minutes. To microwave, thinly slice 4 carrots. Toss with 2 tbsp orange juice or water. Microwave, covered, on high, from 5 to 8 minutes. Stir partway through.

Nutrients: High in vitamin A and fibre.

CORN

Buying: Buy as fresh as possible because corn's natural sugar begins changing into starch as soon as corn is picked.

Storing: Leave husks on and store in coldest part of refrigerator. Use quickly.

Cooking: Remove the husks and cook in boiling water, from 3 to 8 minutes. To microwave 4 ears, remove the silks but leave the husks intact and place the corn cobs in a microwave-safe dish in one layer. Cook, uncovered, on high, from 4 to 8 minutes. Turn once.

Nutrients: Good source of vitamin C. Contains a little vitamin A and B.

HERBS

Freshly snipped herbs add a flavor punch to any dish. Fragrant basil is the most popular fresh herb used. Here's some suggestions for its use along with some other favorites:

- Just before serving, scatter a mix of coarsely chopped herbs over soups or stews for an aromatic perk.

- Chop and toss oregano, coriander, basil or dill into pasta or rice salads.

- Finely chop and stir tarragon, chives or coriander into Dijon for a sandwich spread.

- Use in salads or sprinkle over roasted or barbecued vegetables.

- Chop and stir basil, oregano, thyme or rosemary into tomato sauces and salads. Sprinkle over grilled tomatoes.

• Add a handful of coarsely chopped chives, lemon thyme, mint or rosemary into baking powder biscuits, bread doughs, scalloped potatoes, even macaroni and cheese.

Herbs can also be frozen for later use. Swish in cold water to remove any grit. Drain on paper towels and dry thoroughly. Spread on a tray to freeze. Blanching is not necessary. Once herbs are frozen, pack in airtight containers and return to freezer until ready to use.

Peppers

Buying: Pick firm, bright-colored, sweet bell peppers. Sweet peppers are uniformly mild in taste — red and yellow are simply riper varieties of green — while chili peppers vary in their fieriness.

Storing: Store in the refrigerator crisper. Most peppers will keep for one week. Red peppers, however, don't stand up as well as green.

Cooking: Seed and slice. Sauté in a little butter or oil until tender-crisp, from 3 to 4 minutes. For a slightly smoky, sweet flavor, core, slice in half and seed. Place on the barbecue, under the broiler or in the oven until skins blister and scorch, about 18 minutes at 400°F (200°C). To make them easier to peel, place in a paper or plastic bag and seal. After 10 minutes, peel. They're wonderful in salads or atop a grilled cheese sandwich or store in olive oil or in the refrigerator or freeze.

Nutrients: A single red pepper delivers a lot of vitamins A and C for about 20 calories; a green pepper, also about 20 calories, has fewer of these vitamins but more potassium and magnesium.

Tomatoes

Buying: Select uniform-colored unblemished tomatoes that are firm and heavy for their size.

Storing: Never ripen tomatoes on a windowsill. The direct sunlight will cause them to ripen unevenly. Instead, put underripe tomatoes in a brown paper bag with an apple or pear. The fruit gives off a natural ethylene gas that speeds up the ripening process. Store ripe tomatoes at room temperature.

Cooking: Most people slice tomatoes horizontally, but if sliced vertically — from stem end to bottom — they'll retain more juice. To freeze, cut stem ends from ripe unpeeled tomatoes, then freeze tomatoes. Frozen tomatoes can be held under hot running water and skins will slip off. Use in soups, stews and sauces.

Nutrients: Rich in vitamin A, potassium and niacin; and a reasonably good source of vitamin C, iron and protein.

Zucchini

Buying: Choose small light-green or yellow-flecked zucchini that are supple to the touch.

Storing: Store in open plastic bag in refrigerator. Use within one week.

Cooking: Grate and add to curried chicken or vegetable broth for a quick hot or cool soup or add to tomato sauce. After the water is squeezed from the pulp, use in place of carrots in your favorite carrot cake or as a healthy bonus in muffins. Or slice and sauté in garlic butter. To barbecue, slice lengthwise, brush with oil and sprinkle with cumin, then grill until hot.

Nutrients: Great low-calorie source of vitamins A and C, and niacin and potassium.

FALL & WINTER

CABBAGE

Buying: Buy firm heads, heavy for their size, with crisp leaves.

Storing: Store in a plastic bag in the lower part of the refrigerator for several weeks. For longer storage, remove the outer leaves before placing in plastic bag.

Cooking: Remove tough outer leaves. Cut head in wedges, leaving heart intact. Cook, uncovered, in 2 cups boiling water, from 10 to 15 minutes. To microwave, add 2 tbsp water, broth or wine. Microwave, covered, on high, from 7 to 12 minutes, for 1 small head (1 lb/500 g). Stir partway through.

Nutrients: High in vitamin C.

CAULIFLOWER

Buying: Look for a dense head and tightly packed florets. If you see brown spots that have been shaved off, it's a sure sign of aging.

Storing: Cut off leaves and place in a perforated plastic bag. Store in the lower part of the refrigerator or crisper for four or five days.

Cooking: Remove green leaves, cut off steams, cook whole or cut into florets. To microwave, add 2 to 3 tbsp water, cover with plastic wrap and microwave on high, from 4 to 6 minutes for 1 head, about 1 lb (500 g).

Nutrients: High in vitamin C and potassium. Also contains a reasonable amount of protein and iron.

EGGPLANTS

Buying: Choose smooth-skinned firm eggplants, heavy for their size. Lighter weights may be spongy. Smaller eggplants are often sweeter. Slim narrow or tiny pear-shaped eggplant have sweet flesh and tender skins that don't need to be peeled.

Storing: Store in vegetable bin up to one week or wrap in damp towel and refrigerate for three or four days.

Cooking: Boil or steam 1-in. (2.5-cm) cubes for 5 minutes. Or brush ½-in. (1-cm) slices with oil and broil or barbecue 5 minutes per side.

Nutrients: A good source of folic acid and potassium.

GARLIC

Buying: Choose plump, firm and unshrivelled heads.

Storing: Store, unpeeled, in a cool dry airy place, not the refrigerator and not in a bag. They should stay fresh for weeks.

Cooking: Aroma and flavors aren't released until a clove is chopped, cracked or mashed. When heated, garlic becomes mild, almost buttery, and a score or more of cloves can appear in a single recipe. Boil several cloves with potatoes. Squeeze soft garlic from peel, mash with a fork and stir into mashed potatoes for unbeatable flavor.

MUSHROOMS

Buying: Choose mushrooms that are clean, firm and unblemished. Caps should be a uniform color and tightly closed. As mushrooms mature, they darken in color, the caps open and their flavor intensifies.

Storing: Store in refrigerator, unwashed, in a ventilated paper bag. Use within five days. Oyster and enoki mushrooms are quite delicate, so use within a day of purchasing.

Cooking: When ready to use, wipe with a damp cloth. Do not scrub, peel or soak in water. To sauté, add mushrooms to a frying pan coated with a little butter or oil. Stir constantly over high heat just until you can smell them.

Nutrients: Good source of niacin and low-calorie source of potassium.

PARSNIPS

Buying: Choose firm and smooth roots that are not too large.

Storing: Store in plastic in the refrigerator for up to several weeks.

Cooking: Peel and slice. Place in water with lemon juice to prevent darkening. Add to stews, steam like carrots, mash or french fry like potatoes or roast with other vegetables.

Nutrients: An excellent source of folacin and potassium.

POTATOES

Buying: Choose firm smooth potatoes without sprouts, discoloration or soft spongy spots.

Storing: Do not keep under the sink. Store new potatoes in refrigerator up to one week; others in a cool dry, dark ventilated area for months.

Cooking: Scrub and leave skins on. They contain nutrients and fibre. Prick potatoes, oil and bake at 375°F (190°C), from 50 to 60 minutes. To microwave, pierce and place on a paper towel. For one potato, microwave, on high, 4 minutes. For each additional potato, add 2 to 3 minutes. To boil, cover with water. Boil gently, partially covered, until tender when pierced with a fork, from 25 to 35 minutes.

Nutrients: High in vitamin C and fibre.

SQUASH AND PUMPKIN

Buying: Choose hard shell, free from soft spots.

Storing: Store in cool dry place.

Cooking: For easy cutting, microwave whole, from 1 to 2 minutes. Slice in half and remove seeds. Brush 4 acorn squash halves with butter and bake at 375°F (190°C) from 45 min. to 1 hour. To microwave, pierce skin with a knife to allow steam to escape. Microwave whole, uncovered, from 10 to 15 minutes for 1 large whole 2 lbs (1 kg) squash or pumpkin.

Nutrients: Squash, as well as pumpkin and sweet potatoes, are rich in beta-carotene and antioxidants.

TURNIPS

Buying: Look for fairly small, firm young turnips with few scars and roots.

Storing: Store in a plastic bag in the refrigerator crisper and use within ten days.

Cooking: Cut turnip in thick slices and peel. Dice and cook in ½ in. (1 cm) boiling water or apple juice from 10 to 12 minutes.

Nutrients: Source of potassium. Greens are rich in vitamins A and C and calcium.

SEASONAL GUIDE

YEAR-ROUND

BEANS

Avoid soft, broken or wrinkled dried beans. Pick ones that are uniform in color and shape. Most varieties of beans are available, already cooked, in cans. Drain and rinse before using.

Black Beans
Oval-shaped, small and black-skinned, these firm-textured beans are great in salads, with rice or puréed to make black bean soup.

Chickpeas
This small, heart-shaped, tan-colored bean is also known as garbanzo. Add to soups and stews or use as a base for hot curries. Rich in calcium and iron.

Kidney Beans
These large, kidney-shaped beans are available in red or white. Red kidney beans are traditionally added to chili while white kidney beans are used in soups. Rich in calcium and iron.

Lima Beans
This large, flat, kidney-shaped bean is great in soups or added with kidney beans to chili. Rich in vitamin C and niacin.

GRAINS

Grains are the ripened seeds or fruits of grasses. Most grains such as bulgur and rice will keep for about a year when stored in a tightly covered container in a cool, dry place. However, whole oats and wild rice have a higher oil content and should be stored in the refrigerator or freezer to preserve freshness.

Barley
This dense sweet grain is perfect for soups and pilafs. However, it requires a longer cooking time than most grains because of its denseness.

Bulgur
Bulgur or cracked wheat consists of tiny, tan-colored, irregularly shaped wheat nuggets that are precooked and cracked. They have a robust roasted wheat flavor.

Cornmeal
Cornmeal is a yellow or white flour produced when corn is crushed or ground. Use it to make muffins, breads and polenta.

Couscous
Couscous, a pale golden, granular grain, is a staple of North African cuisine. It is another name for semolina, the milled centre of durum wheat.

Millet
A cereal grass, millet has a delightful nutty smell and taste. An excellent source of fibre, it is also a moderate source of protein. Whole millet can be cooked like rice, made into a pilaf or breakfast cereal, or even brewed into beer! Millet flour is used in flatbreads and cakes.

Oats
Oats are a great source of soluble and insoluble fibre. Soluble fibre lowers cholesterol while insoluble aids in digestion.

Quinoa
Quinoa (pronounced KEEN-wah) is the seed of a plant that originated in the Andes. It's very high in vitamin B and E, as well as phosphorus, and comes packed with enough amino acids to be labeled a complete protein.

Rice

There are three kinds of rice grains — long, medium and short.

- Long-grain rice produces separate fluffy grains when cooked and is great for soups and pilafs. The fragrant basmatic rice, grown in the foothills of the Himalayas and Pakistan, is a long-grain rice that improves with age.

- Medium-grain and short-grain rice tend to stick together when cooked, making them better suited to puddings, rice rings and risottos. Arborio rice, the thick, stubby Italian-style rice, falls into this category.

Wild Rice

Wild rice isn't exactly a rice, but the seed of an aquatic grass related to the rice plant. Although delicious, wild rice is labor-intensive to harvest, so it tends to be expensive.

OLIVE OILS

All olive oils have about 125 calories and 14 g fat per tablespoon. They are generally sold under the following labels:

Extra Virgin Olive Oil

This is the finest olive oil, obtained from the first cold pressing of olives. Fruity and flavorful, often with a deep green-gold or even emerald hue, these oils often command premium prices. Use in dishes where a robust olive taste is important, such as salads and pastas and for dipping bread.

Olive Oil

A blend of refined olive oils is mixed with some extra virgin olive oil to restore the flavor lost in the refining process. With a taste redolent of olives and a golden color, this is the everyday oil used in Mediterranean countries. Use for everyday cooking.

Light Olive Oil

This is a blend of olive oils so refined that it is almost tasteless. The "light" refers to the flavor, not the calories. It is very pale in color. Use in recipes where an olive taste is not needed, such as coleslaw or a stir-fry.

Storing

If you buy more oil than you can use in a couple of months, pour small quantities into opaque bottles for daily use. Store remainder, sealed in original container, in the refrigerator for up to one year.

PASTA

There are more than 50 shapes of pasta from wagon wheels to ear-shaped (orecchiette). The key to cooking great pasta is lots of water. For every pound of pasta, use 4 quarts of cold water. Once water comes to a full rolling boil, add 2 teaspoons salt. Wait for water to boil again. Then add all pasta at once and stir with a wooden spoon. Cook, uncovered, stirring every few minutes. There's no need to add oil to the water. It will make noodles slippery, preventing a sauce from clinging. For al dente or "firm to the bite" consistency, dried pasta takes 7 to 12 minutes to cook; fresh pasta, 1 to 4 minutes. Remember that because the water is extremely hot, pasta will continue cooking while being drained. As soon as pasta is almost cooked, pour it into a colander. Do not rinse with cold water if you are serving pasta hot. Immediately transfer the pasta to a warm serving dish and coat it lightly with your favorite sauce.

INDEX

Look for these titles in the CHATELAINE library

Food Express Series

NEW TWISTS for
100 everyday foods
from apples to zucchini.
Includes a survival guide and
a comprehensive index.

INCLUDES a special section on
off-beat grilling such as pizza,
cornish hens and jambalaya.
Plus indoor adaptations for
year-round sizzle.

INCLUDES favorite recipes
frequently requested by
CHATELAINE readers. Plus
a large section devoted
entirely to chocolate.

Home Decor Series

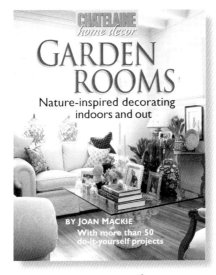

DECORATING INSPIRATION for every room
of the house, including rooms for
outdoor living and dining, with more
than 50 easy do-it-yourself projects.

SOFT MEETS SLEEK, antiques mingle with
contemporary and personal pleasure
combines with comfort in the second book
in the CHATELAINE HOME DECOR series.

CHATELAINE food express
Quickies 2

FOR SMITH SHERMAN BOOKS INC.

EDITORIAL DIRECTOR
Carol Sherman

ART DIRECTOR
Andrew Smith

SENIOR EDITOR
Bernice Eisenstein

ASSOCIATE EDITOR
Erik Tanner

PAGE LAYOUT AND COMPOSITION
Joseph Gisini

COLOR SEPARATIONS
T-C4 Graphics Ltd., Winnipeg

PRINTING
Kromar Printing Ltd., Winnipeg

SMITH SHERMAN BOOKS INC.
533 College Street, Suite 402,
Toronto, Canada M6G 1A8
e-mail: bloke@total.net

FOR CHATELAINE

FOOD EDITOR
Monda Rosenberg

ASSOCIATE FOOD EDITOR
Marilyn Bentz Crowley

TEST KITCHEN ASSISTANT
Trudy Patterson

SENIOR COPY EDITOR
Deborah Aldcorn

CHATELAINE ADVISORY BOARD
Rona Maynard, Lee Simpson

PROJECT MANAGER
Cheryl Smith

SPECIAL SALES
Mark Jones

CHATELAINE, MACLEAN HUNTER PUBLISHING LIMITED
777 Bay Street,
Toronto, Canada M5W 1A7
e-mail: letters@chatelaine.com

ILLUSTRATIONS by Jeff Jackson

PHOTOGRAPHS:

William Deacon: page 21

Michael Mahovlich: front cover and pages 8, 15, 17, 23, 25, 27, 29, 39, 55, 69, 73, 81, 83, 89, 95, 99, 101, 113

Ed O'Neil: pages 2, 11, 31, 35, 41, 43, 45, 49, 53, 61, 87, 93, 103, 107, 111, 115, 119, 123, 127

Michael Visser: pages 67, 77